# WHERE GOD LEADS
# HE PROVIDES

# WHERE GOD LEADS
# HE PROVIDES

## ISAAC ADDAI-DWOMOH

authorHOUSE®

*AuthorHouse*™
*1663 Liberty Drive*
*Bloomington, IN 47403*
*www.authorhouse.com*
*Phone: 1-800-839-8640*

*Published by AuthorHouse    07/20/2012*

*ISBN: 978-1-4772-1897-6 (sc)*
*ISBN: 978-1-4772-1898-3 (hc)*
*ISBN: 978-1-4772-1899-0 (e)*

To my loving wife, Comfort, who out of the love that many come to in the knowledge of the Lord Jesus Christ, encouraged me to write this book. Her desire that many would read, understand, and be a blessing by the Lord Jesus Christ can never be underestimated. May the good Lord richly bless and sustain her in every aspect of her life.

Also to my daughter, Abigail, who read through the manuscript and insisted on its publication. May his light continue to shine in her life. May she come to the knowledge of the revelation of the Lord soon to come, and may she be sustained in all her endeavours in this life.

# CONTENTS

# INTRODUCTION

We are living in a world today where everything seems to be moving very fast. The impact of computers and the Internet cannot be underestimated. Changes are happening in the world every day, and life is constantly changing. Are these changes for the better or worse? Instant coffee, instant tea, instant chocolate, quick fit and instant money. Fast food, fast drink, fast cars, the fast lane, and fast trains.

*Rush* is the key word of the day, not only among the men of this world but also in the Christian community. What do I mean? We don't become Christians overnight as we termed it, as born again believers, instant bleeders, new creatures, and on the spot Christians. They visit the church, respond to an altar call, and when the preacher prays for them, they think, *Bingo! I have made it. I am a Christian, and I am born again.* But it takes more than an altar call to be a Christian. It takes more than a day to know someone. It takes more than an altar call to tell someone to walk closer with the saviour. Man's perspective about God in this day and age has changed. Knowledge seems to abound with the computer age, but the desire to know Christ the creator has diminished. What is happening here? Are we living in the end time spoken of by Daniel the prophet? The time when knowledge increases and many will run to and fro, but the love of many grows cold?

We are living in a world today where we do not need to take things at face value. There is more to life than the eye and ear can meet.

I want to be first, no matter whose toes I tread on. 'Me first and nothing can stop me' has become the mantra of the day. We are dancing ourselves lame even before the main dance begins. Why don't we stop, look, and listen. There is more to life than food and drink. Time is money and it is precious, but rushing is not the answer to our question of life. There is more hope than what the world is offering us and more to life than what the leaders of nations are offering.

Many tend to seek healing instead of the healer. Most people go to church today seeking healing and easily give up after a short time. Even those who receive it quit soon after. Why?

There are some also who seek the provisions of this life—houses, cars, money, properties, clothing, etc.—and once they get them, they think it was by their own power. Some too think that because they are religious they are therefore right before God. If they fall short of these things, then they adopted a negative attitude towards their belief in God and the Church as a whole. Is it not because we don't have the provider or don't know him altogether? We seek comfort instead of the comforter, and we end up burnt out, with nothing in us, more frustrated than ever.

Many are running away from the Church, and many feel so scared to join it. Why? Is there a true God? If so, how do we come to him, walk with him, talk to him, and then hear from him? Is Christianity today what the Bible says it should be? What happens to us when we make Christ our personal saviour and Lord? This book, *Where God Leads, He Provides,* will help you to realise the advantages of the believer's walk with God. Get to know who you are, and your God will provide you with all the necessities of the Kingdom of his dear son.

Men for years have been running their own races and fighting their own battles, but when they fall flat on their faces, they then turn around to blame God. When are we going to learn? We need to take the right turn to meet God. Life and death have been set before us; the choice is ours. So have ignorance and knowledge, joy and calamity, riches and poverty, peace and war, light and darkness, health and sickness, provision and poverty. But in all these things the choice will always remain yours, not God's. God has given man the power to choose. You should always remember that God does not override our will. He has given us our free will to make our own choices. He never treats us like robots.

It is therefore time to quit blaming God for the things we see happening around us and in our lives. Let us check our own lives first and make adjustments where necessary. Our choices will determine our fate. If we walk and work with God, we become winners and our lives and our world will be sharpened But if we choose our own ways and walk where we like, we are then solely responsible for what happens to us and our world.

Let us turn to the book of Deuteronomy 28:1-2(KJV), which says, 'And it shall come to pass, if thou shall hearken diligently unto the voice of the Lord thy God, to observe and to do all his commandment which I command thee this day, that the Lord thy God will set thee on high above all nations of the earth. And all these blessings shall come on thee, and overtake thee, if thou shall hearken unto the voice of the Lord thy God.' Moses made it clear to us that obedience to the word of God will bring blessings and not curses. He says it is blessings that will come on us. Those who observe and then do the will of God shall see blessings overtake them.

When we continue to read through to the fourteenth verse, we see God saying that we shall be blessed not only in the big cities but also in the fields, those remote areas of our lives. In both the field and the city things may happen, situations will arise, trials and difficulties may come, but in all these, those who observe and do the will of God will be blessed. We will be blessed in both the fruit of our body and the fruit of our ground, cattle and sheep. Our baskets and our stores shall be blessed. There shall always be provisions in abundance for you. Whatsoever you set your hands to do shall be blessed.

Enemies will rise against you, but the promise is that God will cause them to be smitten before you. They will come one way, but they will flee from you seven other ways. Why? Because you observe and do the will of God the Father, who is in heaven, the God who created the heavens and the earth.

We hear of famine and drought, earthquakes and floods, fires and storms of destruction, and the only conclusion we hear is that it is God who has caused the heavens not to give rain, who has turned the earth to powder and dust, who has caused nations to be stricken with famine and death. Numerous other reasons can be given for nature's destruction of nations.

Can we sincerely point to God and say, 'Yes, that was God'? What is the promise made to us, those who obey and do the will of God with all earnestness? Does the Bible not say that the Lord shall open unto you his good treasure, the heavens to give rain unto the land in his season, that he shall bless all the work of your hands, that there shall be abundance of food for yourself and other nations that come to thee? Do not the same scriptures promise that no evil shall come near our dwellings? The Lord's abundant blessings shall cause us to lend to many and never borrow.

These are the Lord's words, not the lying words of men. God faithfully does all he has promised, without fail. All his promises are yes and Amen. With faith and patience we will receive the promise. Sit back, check out, think, and also relent when things go wrong. It is not sin to think, for that is the purpose of the mind, but to draw false conclusions due to lack of knowledge is sin and suicidal. If you lack the wisdom and the knowledge of the situation at hand, ask God and he will give you the insight.

Remember that you will never hear God saying one thing today and another tomorrow. God never contradicts himself. His promises to those who will walk in obedience have always been the same. They shall be the head and not the tail, above and not beneath. I don't even sit down to think about failure, because I am destined not to fail. I am a winner. I am successful and prosperous. I am victorious. For all my needs are in his supply. I do aim at the upward calling of God, to receive his grace unto myself, and I look unto Jesus, who is the author and finisher of my faith.

Deuteronomy 7:12-13 (KJV) says, 'Wherefore it shall come to pass, if ye hearken to these judgments, and keep and do them, that the Lord thy God shall keep unto thee the covenant and the mercy which he swore unto thy fathers: And he will love thee, and bless thee, and multiply thee: he will also bless the fruit of thy womb, and the fruit of thy land, thy corn, and thy wine, and thine oil, the increase of thy kine, and the flock of thy sheep, in the land which he swear unto thy fathers to give thee.'

God has promised all obedient children both love and blessing. But when it doesn't come to us we turn to blame him. Why? Are we living in the obedience of his word? Why make a promise at all if God is unable to keep it? Remember, God is God, not man, and he will forever remain God. What he promises, he is able to deliver. So do not let what you see, feel, hear, say, and think distract your focus from the promises God made you. We have been made to be leaders in the things that God has made. In our leadership we need to take responsibilities for all the things that happen around us.

War, famine, storms, earthquakes, suffering, and death are inevitable. These will always be the responsibility of man. The way you act will determine the way things will happen. Your decision—for better or worse, for blessing or curse, for abundance or lack, for peace or war, for rain in its season or drought—will always be yours.

Man has been given authority to rule, tend, and keep all things under heaven. It is therefore time for man to take his position and do the job that that has been assigned to and is required of him.

# CHAPTER 1

## *The If and Why Questions*

The world has witnessed turbulent storms that swept the coast of America and the Caribbean, fires in Australia, floods in Great Britain and Mozambique, which swept the eastern lands of the African continent, the unending flow of blood that has kept that continent in disarray due to wars and rumours of wars, famine and hunger, which have rendered many Africans homeless. The death of children and women in Africa, America, Asia, Europe, Australia, and the Middle East is now inevitable. The most recent uprising has disrupted the Middle East and North African with unending streams of blood. The 'if' and 'why' questions have become very prominent in the lives of many.

The question on the minds and lips of most people is 'If there is a God, why all these atrocities? Why are so many children dying of hunger and famine? Why all the injustice, killing, wickedness, selfishness, and insanity? Why are many living in fear and insecurity, disease and poverty? Why do the rich and powerful overrule the poor and the weak? There seems to be no hope for humanity. Many men and women are going through an unending stream of suffering. Why? If there is a God, can't he do something about it? Why is there no peace here on earth today?

You will surely agree that these questions sound familiar. They are the same questions from the streets of Accra to Zanzibar, from Budapest to Vienna, from Canberra to Jakarta, from Dakar to Tokyo, from Estonia to Patagonia, and from Guatemala to Washington, DC. The same questions are being asked over and over again.

Let us sit back a second and ask ourselves a very simply question. Are we going to question, blame, or deny God's love and his existence just because of the things that we see, hear, and feel in this world of ours today? Can we answer the question of this life genuinely rather than drawing conclusions? Remember you cannot deny a very important issues of this life. It is easy to blame someone if you don't know and have the answers to the problems. Just for a moment try to answer the big question for yourself. You will not get the answers by simply blaming and pointing the finger at someone rather than yourself. Answers to the 'if' and 'why' questions are actually within reach. Relax and put on your seatbelt, and take this journey with me through the issues of this life to find the answers.

First, we need to know who we are. Second, we need to know who our maker is. Finding our identity will enable us to understand why things happen. This begins with finding our roots. Our roots are in Christ, the anointed one. If we are able to locate our identity in Christ, then we will truly know who we are. Do we live and move and have our being in someone else or in ourselves? In whom do we depend, trust, and confide? We can only accept the answers that come from the individual or things in which we depend, trust, and confide.

It is difficult to understand what goes on around us without knowing the source, and why they come upon us. Remember, we are not here by chance. Things do not happen by chance either. There are reasons and answers to every situation that happens upon this earth. My only tip for this generation is to find our identity in Christ Jesus. It is only when we are rooted and grounded in

Christ that we will understand the turbulences, the earthquakes, the floods, the fires, and the storms of this life. God is always in control of situation. Nothing goes unnoticed under the all seeing eyes of God.

Your quest will begin with knowing God. Your understanding of the word of God and his nature will bring you to the place where you will know more about this life.

Your journey to understanding the course of this life begins, therefore, with the word of God. Entrance to his word will bring life and enlightenment. Where there is light, there is revelation; and where there is darkness, there is ignorance. We blame God not because we know but because we are ignorant and don't understand. The fear and the knowledge of the Lord is the beginning of wisdom and revelation. If we lack wisdom, we need to ask the Lord and he will give it to us. I just want you to come to that place where the revelation knowledge of Christ abounds more and more in your life. It is here that one can have the freedom and life through the son, the love of the Father, and the power of the Holy Spirit. I trust the Holy Spirit to enlighten your heart and mind so you are able to come and know him. Knowledge brings revelation when wisdom and understanding are applied.

## Authority Given to Man

Genesis 1:26 makes it clear: '*Man was created in the image and likeness of God. After that God said let them have dominion over the fish of the sea and over the fowl of the air, and over the cattle and over all the earth and over every creeping thing that creeps upon the earth.*'

The first light, which needs to shine on your life, is to know that God made the heaven and the earth and everything in them. Also, both man and woman were created in the image and likeness of God himself. We were also given authority to keep and tend to everything that was made. If we were therefore made to have dominion over everything that was made (i.e., to be caretakers), why do we then blame God when things go wrong? Who has to take authority? Man or God? Who was given dominion over all things? Man or God? Who has to feed, clothe, and house the poor, the homeless, and the destitute? Is it not you and me? Who is it that is polluting the earth and the atmosphere, God or you and me? Is it God who is asking the nations to fight and engage in wars? Why do we blame God and not accept responsibility? If we want to lead, then we need to take responsibility.

We have become irresponsible stewards of the things entrusted into our care. The question is, 'Are we acting in ignorance or irresponsibly?' Have we forgotten who we are, or do we simply not know? We have been going to and fro, not knowing where we are going. If you don't know where you are going, any road will lead you there. If you don't know why things happen the way they do, shut up or find out rather than criticising others or blaming God. God spoke through the prophet Hosea in chapter 4:6: *that for lack of knowledge my people are destroyed*. Where there is illumination there is knowledge.

Is it not because we don't know our identity that we groan, murmur, and complain? We need to understand who we are in the sight of God, and his purposes for our lives. God will always be God and will always remain the same. In the book of Malachi, he says, 'I change not.' Yes! He is the same yesterday, today, and forever. You and I may change, the things of this world may change, and our situation may change, but God never changes. God will always remain omnipotent, omniscient, and omnipresent.

Remember, the amount grain destroyed each year in Europe and the United States alone can feed the whole of Africa, eradicating famine. There are so many natural resources for the whole world to use, but due to improper distribution, through trade sanctions, some countries lack whilst others have more than enough. There was enough informed information to save the lives of many thousands of people who died in the tsunami disaster in Asia. But due to social, political, and economic paralysis among nations, this intelligence was not applied. In the end it was the innocent who suffered. If we don't want the authority God has given us because we cannot fulfil our responsibility, then we need to ask God to take it back. But let me remind you that those who carry on their God-given responsibilities always see his glory in their lives. For where God leads, he also provides.

# CHAPTER 2

## *Who Is Man?*

This is a question that few men can answer. Finding your identity is the first part of your knowledge and blessings. Get to know your identity before you ask questions. Don't blame God and others when a thing does not happen the way you want.

You and I were made in the image and likeness of God. Looking at the Genesis account of creation, we come to realise that man was made after God spoke him into being, just as with other things God created. That creative power is also in man. Man can come to this revelation only if he realises his identity.

Do we realise that God is the giver of life? Do we depend on him for our fullness of life? Nothing can make men give except what he has already received or given. Take it or leave it, you can and will always give what you are given. There is nothing under heaven that man can take credit for. Not knowing who he is, man has turned to being destructive instead of creative.

Who are we at all? Are we just passing through, or do we have an important job to do here on earth? Our job is to tend and to keep. God is the giver of life. It is from him that life and greatness come. In his life we have life. Outside God there is death and destruction. John makes plain to us the things that Jesus said:

John 10:10: *'The thief comes not but to steal and to kill and to destroy. I have come that they might have life and have it in abundance.'*

Life in its fullness is only from God. This life kind of 'life' in the Greek means 'Zoe', and it only comes to those who make the Lord their Shepherd. The sheep are those who hear his voice and follow him, those who are willing to obey God. Death does not belong to those who find their identity in Christ.

John 15:1-2 says, *'I am the true vine and my father is the husbandman. Every branch in me that bears no fruit he takes away and every branch that bears fruit, he purges that it may bring forth more fruit.'(KJV)* If we are looking for the supernatural in this world of ours today, we need to come to our identity. We need the vines as branches to come to our fullness of bearing much fruits. Where there is no vine there is no branch, just as there are no fruits without the branches. If we were to go to Old Testament times and look at the three most important pieces of furniture found in the holy place of the Tabernacle, we would understand our identity better: the table of showbread, the altar of incense, and the candle stick. This candlestick had six branches, shaft, knaps, and flowers. It was from the shaft that the oil, which feeds the whole candlestick, passes, and without the oil the branches will not give light.

The whole candlestick is God, the shaft is Jesus, and the oil is the Holy Spirit. The branches are believers. The only way the branches or believers can give out lights is the oil of the Holy Spirit coming through the shaft, or Christ. The Holy Spirit worked together with us to enable us live a fulfilled life. Man by himself can do nothing; by himself cannot make it. With God on our side, we can do all things.

Man's life depends on that which comes from God. There is no life outside God for the man or woman who does not know God. In his life we have life. He is the source of our life and our supply.

This is why those without God are said to be dead, even though they live. They are the branches hanging dead on the tree with no sustenance. Without the needed sustenance and nourishment they drop from the vine and lose their place altogether. Remember that there can be no branch outside the vine.

Your identity depends on who you are. I have never seen any orange branch sitting on top of an apple vine. Neither have I seen an avocado tree bring forth oranges. 'We shall be known by our fruit.' Matthew 7:16a

Let us for a second look at Jesus' prayer in John 14:16, which says, *'And I will pray the father and he shall give you another comforter, that he may abide with you forever.'* The word comforter in Greek is *paraklesis*, which means 'helper', or 'one called alongside to help'. When you count God out of your system, there will be no life for you.

In finding our identity we need to know how to cleanse, abide, and obey. These are three main conditions of fruit bearing. In John 15:2; 4; *10 Jesus said "every branch in me that bears not fruit he takes away and every branch that bear fruit he purges that it bear more fruit. Abide in me, and I in you. As the branch cannot bear fruit of itself, except it abide in the vine; No more can ye, except ye abide in me. If you keep my commandment you shall abide in my love; even as I have kept my Father's commandments, and abide in his love."* The men and women who take all their burdens and cares to him receive all wisdom, life, and strength from him. Our cleansing, abiding, and total obedience bring our success in life. Your blessing or curses in life, will depend on how much you depend on God.

Psalms 91:1 says, *'He who dwells in the secret place of the most high shall abide under the shadow of the Almighty.'* The level to which you depend on God will determine the level to which you are protected. Do you abide or inhabit in the secret place of God? If so he will hide you in his Tabernacle and set you upon a rock.

Where do you find your identity? Is it in Christ Jesus our Lord? If so, terror, pestilence, darkness, destruction, and arrows will come but will not be able to overcome you. A thousand shall fall at your side, and ten thousand at your right hand, but it shall not come near you. Only with your eyes shall you behold the reward of the wicked.

Who is the 'wicked' the Psalmist is referring to? Is he not the individual who does not have his identity in Christ? I have in the past believed that as soon as you come to the Lord, it will be bread and butter, milk and honey, on the table at all times. I have thought it will be eternal summer camp, where you eat, play, and sleep, a trouble-, war- and devil-free zone. But I have grown over the years to realise that this is not the case.

The scripture makes it clear to us that 'many are the affliction of the righteous; but the Lord shall bring deliverance.' Psalms 34:19' Remember deliverance comes to those who have their identity in Christ.

Let us look at Psalms 91:9-10 and 13, (KJV) which says, 'Because thou have made the Lord which is my refuge, even the most high thy habitation; There shall no evil before thee neither shall any plague come near thy dwelling. Thou shall tread upon lion and adder, the young lion and the dragon shall thou trample under feet.'

This passage speaks to the individual who abides in God, whose life and being is solely dependent on God at all times. The degree of your dependents, the degree of your trust, and the degree of your confidence will determine the degree of your receiving from the Lord.

Jesus puts it in very simple language in John 15:7: *'If you abide in me, and my words abide in you, you will ask anything that you want and it shall be done unto you.'* Those who abide give their will totally to God and adhere to the word of God. They are those people whose lives depend solely on the Lord and his words, knowing that life outside the word of God is death. They are those whose lives depend on the word no matter what their situation. The man and woman who abide in Christ don't give up but always stand firm. He or she never turns his or her back on the word.

Depending on the word of God brings to mind an incident that occurred at Gatwick Airport in the United Kingdom in March 1986. At this time the devil tried to hinder us, knowing what the good Lord was going to accomplish in our lives. Even though our travel particulars were intact, we were detained for several hours for no apparent reason. We were interviewed one after the other. I really know what standing on the word of God can achieve. After our interrogation, we were left on our own for some time, so I asked my travelling companion to join me in prayer. There is power behind the word of God. We prayed for the supernatural intervention of God in this situation. The word of God makes it clear to us that 'the effectual fervent prayer of the righteous man availeth much' James 5:16. Our prayers were not hindered; there was an intervention, for God is a prayer-answering God.

After our prayers there was an instant apology from the immigration officials. They said that there had been a misunderstanding in the information they gathered regarding our invitations. You know what? I did rejoice for that quick answer to our prayer. Dear reader, the word of God works. It is alive and it is quick, and it is real. I can enthusiastically depend on it, and so can you. It never fails. Let it dwell in you richly.

Psalms 91:14-16 continue to say, 'Because he has set his love upon me therefore will I deliver him; I will set him on high because he has known my name. He shall call upon me, and I will answer him, I will be with him in trouble. I will deliver him and honor him. With long life will I satisfy him and show him my salvation.' The Psalmist explains how God is ready to satisfy us if we are ready to stand and depend on his word. How far are we prepared to go with the Lord on his word? We can't separate the Lord from his word.

In John 1:1 we read, *'In the beginning was the word and the word were with God and the word was God.'* The word is God himself. The more we depend on the word, the more of God's intervention we have in our situation. How much of God's word do you have in your system? What is your level of faith in the word of God? Most people get confused when they talk about faith. Your faith is your confidence, conviction, reliance, dependence, and level of trust in the word of God. Having faith in the word of God depends on the amount of God's word you have learnt, known, and applied. You can't become a doer of the word until you know the word, and you can't know the word until you have learned or studied it.

Paul wrote to the Philippians (4:9 KJV), saying, *'Those things, which ye have both learned, and received and heard and seen in me do, and the God of peace shall be with you.'* Paul was able to do the things, which he has learned and known. Just as a doctor, an engineer, a carpenter, an electrician, an economist, or a nurse can also do only those things that they have spent their time and energy learning and knowing. It is my pleasure that you all come to the knowledge of his word and to do all that he has commanded you, for the release of his blessing in your life.

Yes, you are the man that God made in his own image and after his likeness for his own glory. Man was made for the purpose of keeping God's word, to enable his power to manifest through your life.

# CHAPTER 3

## *He Breaks Our Curse*

In every area of our life where God leads, he makes provision for us. But the question is, 'Have you found your identity in Christ?' Have you found your refuge in God? Do you actually dwell in the secret place of the most high? Is God thy shield and great reward. As he said to Abraham, remember, until you come to the very place where your identity is in Christ Jesus, you cannot come to the full revelation of God, where you can receive the goodness of God in your life.

You may be seeking healing or a breakthrough in your business, but it is not forthcoming. Things may have turned upside down. Life may have become unbearable, all heaven broken loose on you. Friends and relatives seem to be against you and are always discouraging you. You are disliked, disowned, unloved, and uncared for. Whatever you do seems to be criticised. Your personality is shattered by disease and sickness. Your entire life seems inferior. Your life and marriage are in shambles. Your finances may be crippled. Your life may be a matter of survival or death. There seems to be no way out of your situation. To the left, right, front, and back, you are entangled. The only question that you are able to asked is 'Why me?' Why who? Have you forgotten that your level of faith determines what you receive? The answers will come from no one except Jesus, the only begotten of the Father.

The scriptures are full of examples of men and women who had their identity in God and then received their breakthrough. Through their faith in God, some were able to subdue the kingdom and obtain promises. Women who received death were raised to life again, and the blind received their sight. Many had their nets broken or their boats sunk. Paralytics came to the place where they received their miracle through faith.

What was their secret? It was the person with whom they identified themselves. Who is your identity? Paul identified himself with Christ—what about you? We need to identify with his death and resurrection. Paul, in writing to the Galatians,chapter 2 verse 20 said, *'I am crucified with Christ nevertheless I live, yet not I, but Christ live in me, and the life which I now live in the flesh I live by faith of the Son of God, who loved me, and gave himself for me.'* *(KJV)* What a thrilling statement! Not only are we loved by God, but he also sent his only son to die for us. If I'm loved by my maker, who can curse me? Who dares come against God's elect? Who dares touch God's anointed, who is in covenant with him?

Paul says in Galatians 3:13-14, 'Christ has redeemed us from the curse of the law, being made a curse for us: for it is written curse is everyone that hangs on a tree: That the blessing of Abraham might come on the Gentile through Jesus Christ, that we might receive the promise of the spirit through faith.' (KJV)

There is so much that God has made available for those who love him, particularly those who are called by his purpose. No matter how many negative pronouncement made against us by the enemy, when we come in covenant with God we are redeemed. Christ himself has become our substitute or surrogate, paying the price for all mankind. When we submit to Jesus, He cancelled the handwritten of ordinances that was against us from the devil, which is contrary to us. He triumph over all principalities and powers, thereby bringing to naught the effects of the devil against the children of God the Father. Not only are we redeemed from the curse of the law, but we are also given the promise of the spirit through faith. What more do we need if God is capable of changing what comes against us? How much more does he have in store for those he loves? Yes, many are the promises of God. When we keep the conditions of God, we always receive the promise. God is always ready to fulfil his part of the bargain. When men remain under God's direction then the promise is fulfilled in their lives. It is only God who is capable of translating us from the curse of the law to his abundant blessing, which he has in store for those who are called according to his purpose.

It is sad to see what people do when they are not happy with their life situation. Man will go the length and breadth of the globe for answers to their situation, but turning to God becomes a big issue. The Church has become a no-go area. The Church is only for the miserable ones who have nothing better to do with their lives. Folks who refuse to participate in the things of this world also refuse to enjoy the things of this world. If men would return to God with all their hearts and minds, then the blessing of Christ would redeem them from curse. Those who, through faith, identified themselves with Christ would always see the glory of God. There is no curse upon those who are in Christ, only blessing. It is the very blessing that God's promised Abraham when he became his covenant partner. God blessed Abraham and all his children, and his children's children, and all those who bless him.

Moses gives us a typical example in the book of Exodus 15:22-26:

*So Moses brought Israel from the red sea, and they went out into the wilderness of Shur; and they went three days in the wilderness, and found no water. And when they came to Marah, they could not drink of the waters of Marah, for they were bitter; therefore the name of it was called Marah. And the people murmured against Moses, saying, what shall we drink? And he cried unto the Lord, and the Lord showed him a tree which when he had cast into the waters the waters were made sweet. There he made for them a statute and ordinance, and there he proved them, and said if thou will diligently hearken to the voice of the Lord thy God, and wilt do that which is right in his sight, and will give ear to his commandments and keep all his statutes, I will put none of these diseases upon thee, which I have brought upon the Egyptians; for I am the Lord that heals thee.(KJV)*

God is the one who is able to turn your curse into blessing, your bitterness into sweetness, your unbearable into bearable. He is the very God who can turn your murmuring to joy and dancing. Not only is God able to change your situation around. It is his nature and his will to do so. It is God's will that you prosper and be in health. It is God's desire that his children get the best in life and live happily.

Why do you think God brought diseases upon the Egyptians? Was it not because they rebelled and had other gods besides the living and only God? Their identity was not found in God. Your faith will surely determine what you receive from God.

In Romans 8:28, Paul says, *'And we know that all things work together for good to them that love God, to them who are the called according to his purpose.'* Paul called to mind the things that God has in store for those who love him. The elect of God, and those who have their identity in Christ, are men and women who are called by his purpose.

Paul continues in verse 31,

What *then shall we say in response to this? If God is for us who can be against us? He who did not spare his own Son, but gave him up for us all, how will he not also, along with him, graciously give us all things? Who will bring a charge against those whom God has chosen? It is God who justifies. Who is he that condemns? Christ Jesus, who died more than that, who was raised to life, is at the right hand of God and is also interceding for us. Who shall separate us from the love of Christ? Shall trouble or hardship or persecution or famine or nakedness or danger or sword? As it is written, for your sake we face death all day long, we are considered as sheep to be slaughtered. No, in all these things we are more than conquerors through him who loved us.(NIV)*

No evil can come before the elect of God. We are freely given all things in this life. That doesn't mean that trails and difficulties will not come. Persecution, famine, distress, nakedness, and peril shall come, but we will be delivered from them all. Just as the book of Psalms says, many are the afflictions of the righteous, but the Lord shall deliver him from them all. We will always be set free and blessed, no matter how numerous our afflictions may be.

Moses helps us to understand this. Deuteronomy 28:14-15 (KJV) says, *'And thou shall not go aside from any of the word which I command thee this day, to the right hand or to the left to go after other gods to serve them. But it shall come to pass, if thou will not hearken unto the voice of the Lord thy God to observe to do all his commandment and his statutes which I command thee this day, that all these curse shall come upon thee and overtake thee.'*

Only those who have the Lord as their God and live in obedience to his word may receive his blessings and live not under a curse. It is the blessing of the Lord, which overtakes us and sets us on high.

Those of us who are trying to make it on our own strength can end up like the man who travelled many days in search of water. In his hunger and weariness he came across a river overflowing at its banks. All this weary individual could do was fill his belly after quenching his thirst. Without proper preparation he could take nothing with him—not even a drop—but had to go back and start all over again. We try so hard, we travel to and from in order to make it, but to no avail. We are fighting a losing battle, and the fight goes on. The blessing of God overflows in those of us who let him work in our life and always prepare for it. The blessing of God sometimes comes when we do not expect it. With faith and patience we will inherit the promise. The word, having its full place in our life, will set us on high, so much so that we will be able to move mountains. Blessings and goodness, not curses and evil, will follow the believer and the individual whose identity is in God.

# CHAPTER 4

## *He Heals Our Diseases and Sickness*

I find it difficult to understand why some people partially accept the Bible and ignore the rest blatantly. I simply attribute this to a lack of knowledge, which God says destroys his people. Many people have not come to the knowledge of God and therefore have suffered greatly by not coming to his revelation. I do believe that most people refuse divine healing not because God can't heal them but because they have not come to the very place where their faith is strong enough to heal them or to receive healing. Don't forget, 'without faith it is impossible to please God', and if none can please God without faith, then it is impossible to receive from God without it.

God is surely a prayer-answering God, to those who truly believe that God is capable of bringing their healing to pass.

Don't expect to be healed if you do not have enough faith for your healing. God is a God of faith. He called things that were not as though they were. God can make things happen, even the impossible. Faith is that element that pulls the powers of heaven to work on our behalf. Our faith in the word of God concerning our sickness and diseases will pull the power of God to bring the health we desire in our lives. It is the word of God that works in our life situation. The book of Leviticus 18:5 says, *'Keep my decrees and laws, for the man who obeys them will live by them.'* No matter how religious you may be, if you do not believe in and adhere to the word of God concerning your healing, you will never receive your healing. We need to know for sure that it is God's perfect will that we his children prosper and live in health. He is the same God who both prospers and heals. If he can cause you to prosper, then he can also heal you and give you peace. I personally don't see God as someone who is always willing to give his people prosperity but not healing. What good is prosperity to you without the necessary health to enjoy the blessing that he has given you? If we are believers, then we need to behave as believers.

This brings us to the issues of salvation. The first and foremost aspect in a believer's life is his salvation. You might as well pack it in if you do not have salvation. It is the key to receiving the gift from God. We can only have the blessing we desire when our salvation is complete. Salvation is a package in the Kingdom. If you leave it, you forgo all the things included in it. In the Greek language, 'soteria' (salvation) includes healing, prosperity, redemption, propitiation, sanctification, and justification.

Paul wrote to the Romans, in chapter 1:16, '*For I am not ashamed of the gospel of Christ, for it is the power of God unto salvation to everyone that believeth, to the Jews first and also to the Greeks.*' ( KJV) This scripture indicates the power that the word of God entails. It has the power to bring to pass our salvation, which also includes our healing. Let God be God through his word. If the word has power to give me salvation, then it equally has the ability to bring to pass my desired health.

## WHAT DOES THE WORD OF GOD SAYS ABOUT MY HEALING?

Exodus 15:26 says, '*And said, If thou will diligently hearken to the voice of the Lord thy God, and will do that which is right is his sight, and will give ear to his commandments, and keep all his statues, I will put none of these diseases upon thee, which I have brought upon the Egyptians, for I am the Lord that Heals thee.' (KJV)*

Our obedience will bring about our healing. If we believe God can and is willing to heal us, then our healing will come. If we deny the power through his word to heal us, then our healing will not come. If we deny the power through his word to heal us, then we will also not receive our healing. Rest assured that God heals and is ready to grant it to everyone who asks him in faith. Faithfulness to his word will surely bring to pass our desired healing and health.

Jesus said in John 10:10, *reads, 'The thief comes only to steal and to kill and destroy, I have come that they may have life, and have it to the full.'* I don't see life in abundance or to the full with sickness and diseases. When God promises to deliver us he always delivers us to the full. If the word says life to the full, it is surely life to the full. It has always been the desire of the enemy to bring us down, to destroy God's people with sickness and disease in order to discourage us in our walk with the Lord. Thank God we have the Lord on our side. If God be for us, who therefore can be against us?

Philippians 4:19 says, *'My God shall supply all my needs according to his riches in glory by Christ Jesus.'* Healing is also a need, and if God is going to supply all my needs then I also accept him to heal my sickness and diseases as well.

For eighteen wonderful years I have lived in perfect health in praise of our soon-to-come King. Just as he heals, he is also capable of keeping us in perfect health and shape.

In 1983, I became very sick to the point of death. Those who saw me at that time will testify of this. I spent so much on hospital bills and medication, but there was little improvement. Due to my worsening condition I even try to double the medication dosage for a quick recovery and to sleep at night, but to no avail. If I did walk it was with the help of someone aiding me. My sight was also affected, and I couldn't see properly. There wasn't much hope in my situation as at that time. Money was also an issue, since I had no income. Medication was not the answer to my situation. It was time to meet the healer and not the healing. It was also time to meet my maker, who knows my flame, for where God leads, he provides.

So much was done by so many loved ones. May my God bless those who through love and compassion offered financial support and friendship to see me through those times. My most thanks goes to Rev. Joseph Akuoko and his dear wife, Mrs. Victoria Akuoko. Both offered spiritual and financial support during those moments. God is always faithful in all things. May you all live to see his faithfulness in your lives. Remember what God has promised; he is capable of bringing it to pass. The Church at that time, realising my condition, also began to pray. The scripture makes it plain that the fervent prayer of the righteous avails much. God is a prayer-answering God who shows no partiality, and he is not a respecter of persons. Those prayers of the faithful brought about the victory desired and the perfect healing I was seeking. Remember, it was not by might or by power but by his spirit. There were times when I needed to spend more time in the word of God and also in prayer.

The fervent prayer based on the word of God brings the results we desire. Let the word of God dwell in your heart and mind richly and you will never be the same. Since my deliverance from sickness my life has never been the same. I have always lived in that perfect health made available for me. Who said God can't heal? Who said God wouldn't heal? I am a living testimony. I don't know your situation or condition with regard to health or healing. It is not what doctors and physicians or friends say but what God is saying about your situation. He did it in the life of a woman who had an affliction of the blood for twelve years, spending all she had. Her contact with Jesus brought about her desired healing. Why not come in contact with your healer?

In John 15:7, Jesus says, '*If you remain in me and my words remain in you, ask whatever you wish, and it will be given to you.*' What a promise that cannot be refused. You can surely bank on it, and it will surely come to pass. This brings to mind a woman we visited who was near the point of death. Her condition was unbearable, looking at her. You could not stand beside her for ten minutes without tears running down your cheeks. That was how serious the woman's condition was. We talked to her and saw her in that condition, and to be honest with you, none of us looking at her saw any natural hope. Yet where there is no way, God can make a way. Remember, when everything surrounding you becomes a shadow over your eyes, know for sure that your redeemer lives. After few months this dear sister revived and her deteriorated condition began to get better and better. Today I say this in praise of our soon-to-come King: this dear sister is living in perfect health. Doctors' diagnoses and medications couldn't save her. Her money couldn't buy the necessary health she desired. The name of Jesus in the prayer of his saints brought results. Who said God cannot and will not heal? Check the scriptures for yourself, and ask for God's will concerning your situation. Let God decide, not manmade doctrine. It is God who has the final word, not man. Let the word of God speak for itself. I am sick and tired of hearing ministers and believers tell others that healing is the thing of the past, that it is not for the Church today. Who are we to decide for God? Is God not the same yesterday, today, and forever? If the lame walked, the blind saw, the dumb spoke, and the dead were raised back to life, he can do the same today.

Remember what God says in Malachi 3:6. *'I am the Lord, I change not.'* If God changes not, why do we try to change him? Live by the word and leave the rest to him. Why do we try to play God and try to put him in a box? Remember, God is God, and he is a big God. You are what you say God is. Yes, you are what you think God is, and you will also become what you picture God to be. I have seen people healed by the power of God. I have also prayed for the sick and have seen them healed by God. I am still waiting to see someone who releases his or her faith and not be healed. I myself have been prayed for and healed. Without reasonable doubt, all the situations and conditions mentioned above were done by God.

## THE LEVEL OF YOUR FAITH DETERMINES THE LEVEL OF YOUR RECEIVING

Where God leads, he surely provides. Your level of faith will always be the deciding factor in receiving from God. This brings to mind a story of a centurion who came to Jesus because his servant lay at home sick of the palsy and grievously tormented of the devil. He did not desire that Jesus come under his roof, thinking he was not worthy, but only speak the word and his servant shall be healed. The centurion's faith was rewarded. Jesus said as he has believed so be it done unto him. The scripture says 'that the servant was healed in the selfsame hour'. The centurion faith releases the power of God to work on his behalf.

Lets take a quick look at Acts 10:38, which says, *'How God anointed Jesus of Nazareth with the Holy Ghost and with power who went about doing good and healing all that were oppressed of the devil for God was with him.'* We here see clearly the work of the devil. He brings sickness, suffering, and difficulties upon us. This is where many turn to blame God for his lack of care, sometimes denying his existence. The very contrast is what the Lord Jesus came to do.

He was anointed by God to do good deeds and to heal all those who were oppressed by the devil. I don't see myself well if I'm sick and diseased. The healing power of Jesus was able to bring health to the lame, blind, crippled, dumb, and mute. Also the paralytic, the lunatic, the crooked, and the dropsy were all healed of Christ Jesus. If the Lord did all of the above in biblical days, be assured he can do it today. Just as he was alive with power in the life of Bartimaeus, so is his power of healing today. He is alive, and with the same power. Death couldn't hold him captive. Even in the grave he was still the Lord. In his resurrection all authority has been given to him. At the name of Jesus every one shall bow, including sickness and diseases, and every tongue shall confess Jesus Christ as our Lord to the praise and glory of the Father.

Malachi 4:2 states, *'But unto you that fear my name shall the sun of righteousness arise with healing in his wings.'*

There is healing in Christ Jesus unto them that fear and trust his name. Your faith is what makes the difference. I just don't understand some people sometimes. We sometimes ignore some of the scriptures concerning the promises of God. But to be honest with you, we are all using the same Bible. 1 Peter 2:24 (KJV) says, "Who his own self bare our sins in his own body on the tree, that we, being dead to sins, should live unto righteousness; by whose stripes ye were healed."

In Jesus' suffering he allowed us who trust in him receive healing. He bore our sins so that in death we might live. Someone capable of giving us life in place of death will he not give us health in place of sickness and diseases. If we are able to release our faith in him, he is capable of releasing our desired health. Who is like unto our God? He is capable of bringing to pass our needs when we ask him. It is in his will. It is within his love. Our health is within the promises of God the Father.

25

Numbers 21:5-9 (KJV) helps us understand the willingness of Jesus to heal us, especially those who walk in faith:

*"And the people spoke against God and against Moses, wherefore have you brought us up out of Egypt to die in the wilderness? For there is no bread, neither is there any water, and our soul loathes this light bread". And the Lord sent fiery serpent among the people and they bit the people and much people of Israel died. Therefore the people came to Moses and said, we have sinned, for we have spoken against the Lord and against thee; pray unto the Lord that he take away the serpent from us. And Moses prayed for the people.*

*And the Lord said to Moses, make thee a fiery serpent, and set it upon a pole, and it shall come to pass that every one that is bitten when he looked upon it shall live. And Moses made a serpent of brass and put it upon a pole and it came to pass, that if a serpent had bitten any man when he be held the serpent of brass, he lived".*

Sin brings death and destruction, for the wage of sin is death. Sin also brings separation between you and your God. Sin hinders our request in our prayer to the Lord. The prophet Isaiah says, *'Behold, the Lord's hand is not shortened, that it cannot save; neither his ear heavy, that it cannot hear. But your iniquities have separated between you and your God, and your sins have hid his face from you, that he will not hear.' Isaiah 59:1,2 (KJV).* Our sins will find us out. Our well of receiving from God will dry up when we sin. Our flow will be disconnected. We sometimes do not receive our healing not because God can't heal or won't heal but because of sin.

If you are expecting healing from the Lord, then I would like you to check your life. If there happens to be any sin in you, confess and repent from it immediately and the good Lord will forgive you. John 1:9 says, "if we confess our sins, he is faithful and just to forgive us our sins and to cleanse us from all unrighteousness."

Make your confession to the Lord and he will forgive you and heal you. When Israel sinned and repented of their sins, they were forgiven and God and made provision for them to receive their healing. The only condition to receiving from God is to respond to God's word and instructions in faith. Israel's instruction was to look up to the brazen serpent, and healing would come forth. Those who became obedient received their healing, but those who doubted died.

Your faith will make the difference between healing and suffering, between life and death. May I also remind you of the fact that seventy percent of the miracles that took place in the Bible at the time of Jesus were the result of the people's faith. Luke makes it clear that the woman with the issue of the blood was made whole by her faith in the Lord. Release your faith and it will work for you. Quit thinking healing is outdated and that it is not the will of God. God is willing and able to heal you. David's prayer in Psalms 103:1-3 NKJV) is your prayer also. *'Bless the Lord O my soul and all that is within me bless his holy name, Bless the Lord, O my soul and forget not his benefits, who forgives all your iniquities, who heals all they diseases.'*

It is my prayer that all believers will see God in the light of his world and not be entangled with the manmade doctrine that easily beset us, the yoke of bondage that imprisons us. Look unto Jesus, who is the author and finisher of your faith. Your faith should not rest in men, but let it rest in the Lord the giver of life. Seek the healer and your healing will be fulfilled. Seek the provider and you will receive your provision. Above all, seek first the Kingdom and its righteousness and all others will be added unto you.

# THE QUESTION OF FAITH

The subject of faith has rested heavily on the minds of many believers for so long a time. As believers our daily walk should be a walk of faith, without which the result would be sin. What is this faith we are talking about? It is the amount of God's word in you to use when the need arises. I would therefore say faith is simply trusting God—the confidence, the assurance, the dependence, and the reliance of God's word in your life as a believer. Is it the whole word of God, which you believe or just part of it?

Paul's second letter to Timothy, chapter 3:16 (KJV), says, '*All scripture is given by inspiration of God, and is profitable for doctrine for reprove, for correction, for instruction in righteousness, that the man of God may be perfect thoroughly furnished unto all good works.*' Those who realise that all scriptures are the word of God and live by them are those who see the glory of God in their lives. God and his word cannot be separated. Faith in the entire word of God brings life and victory. Deny the power in the word of God, and the grace due to you will not materialise. Your faith will see you through and set you on high. Disobey and anarchy strikes. The victory you need is based on the word of God, which you have in your system. Anything outside faith in what the Bible says is sin.

Many sons and daughters of Israel died because they disobeyed God. They did not take God at his word. Those who want to see the supernatural are those who walk in faith. Do you truly want to know why disasters like earthquakes, famine, wars, fires, and floods come about? Is it not because we haven't come to the revelation knowledge of the God? Remember, entrance into his word brings light. We are not in the known because we live in darkness and have no light. We have neglected our responsibilities and duties as subjects of God, and in our ignorance we destroy. It is easy to complain when we see people and nations in danger and being destroyed without checking out the root cause of all these things. Who are we to point fingers at God and accuse him? As creatures we turn to blame God the creator. Our wisdom, understanding, and knowledge of the word of God will bring revelation knowledge. Let the light of God's word shine in your heart and you will never be the same ever again. God is light, and in him there is no darkness.

Ignorance to the word brings death. Some claim to have the revelation of God, but they lack the wisdom of it. When are we going to sit back and study the word so that we will be able to say the right thing at the right time? It is sad to hear the things that some preachers say, pretending to speak for God. Where God leads, he always provides. Where he sends, he guides. When He speaks the word they come to pass. Let the word of God dwell in you, and you will live. Your faith level definitely determines your blessing level or your failure level. Your faith can build or destroy.

The time for faith, which comes by hearing and hearing by the word of God, is now. Without it, all we do would be sin. Paul makes it clear to the Romans that, it is in the gospel that the righteousness of God, is revealed from faith to faith. As it is written in the book of Romans, 'the just shall live by faith'. We have our right standing with God through his word. Have the word of God in you and you will have the mind of Christ.

# CHAPTER 5

## *Where God Leads, He Also Empowers*

Never in my life have I seen so much power invested in the policemen and women in Great Britain. They seem to have more power than any other group, both here and in other countries I have visited round the world. I have been to places under military rule, where the armed forces are in control of the social, economic, and political situation of the country. I was brought up in a place where the soldiers with their guns patrolled the streets of the cities and towns to protect the military regime, ruling by dictatorship to satisfy their selfish ambitions. Without the help of the soldiers they knew they would not succeed, but the police who were supposed to secure law and order had no respect in the role they played in the running of the country's affairs. A country like Britain,which keeps it soldiers in barracks to play their role in society when necessary. They have a better system. They have endowed the police with so many powers and much authority that their role in the society helps to protect not only the favourite few, like the government, but every individual living in the country. Their presence of the police at work will scare the innocent by-stand, not to mention the lawbreakers. They may have no guns, but they have authority.

A policeman on the streets of England wearing a uniform has all the power of her majesty the Queen backing him. However, he cannot do as he pleases but within the rules and regulations. He or she acts in the name of the law, applying the powers given by her majesty the Queen. In her service the policeman has the authority to secure law and order, but outside the force he is an ordinary member of the community, just like everyone else.

Just as the policemen has powers to exercise authority over a given jurisdiction, so does the man or woman who is called by God. Those who are called by God are empowered, and that things work together for their good. God's people have even more power and authority than policemen. Believers have powers and authority that break the bonds of the devil. Principalities, powers, and rulers in the darkness of this world submit to this authority. Therefore the so-called believers out there, who are patrolling the streets with no armour on, should check out why they are there and in whose name they are representing. We are empowered by the Holy Spirit of God to do the work of the ministry. Without the spirit of God inside us, there isn't much we can do.

## The Power of the Holy Spirit in Old Testament Times

Genesis 1:1-2 says, *'In the beginning God created heaven and the earth. The earth was without form and void; and darkness was upon the face of the deep and the spirit of God was moving over the face of the water.'*

According to the account of Moses, the heavens and the earth were created by the 'Elohim', which is a Hebrew for God, a plural noun. The earth was without form and void and darkness was upon the face of the waters. This account helps us to realise the active part the spirit of God played in creation. In the darkness, void, and formlessness of the earth, the spirit of God moved upon the waters to bring to pass the things that God wants to create.

So also was the spirit present in the creation of man. Genesis 1:26 says, *'And God said, let us make man in our own image, after our likeness; and let them have dominion over the fish of the sea, and over the fowls of the air, and over the cattle and, over the earth, and over every creeping thing that creeps upon the earth.'* Chapter 2:7 adds, *'And the Lord God formed man out of the dust of the ground and breathe into his nostrils the breath of life and man became a living soul.'*

The breath of life is part of the God-given spirit that brought life to mankind, in that God is essentially spirit. Therefore, we can say man, who is similar to God, possesses an immortal spirit. It cannot be taken for granted that the breath of life that the Lord God breathed into man's nostrils. Isaiah also declared that 'The Lord God created the heavens and stretched them out.' He that spread forth the earth and all that is in it breathed unto the people upon it, giving the spirit to them that walk therein.

The spirit who took part in creation is also the source of human life. God is the creator who acts in every situation, whether in nature or in history. Born-again believers should note that great gifts and powers are given by the Spirit to do more and exceedingly, just as it happened in the early believers.

Judges 3:9-11 says, *'And when the children of Israel cried unto the Lord, the Lord raised up a deliverer to the children of Israel who delivered them, even Othniel the son of Kenaz, Caleb's younger brother,. And the spirit of the Lord came upon him, and he judged Israel, and went out to war and the Lord delivered Chushan-rishathaim king of Mesopotamia into his hand, and his hand prevailed against Chushan-rishathaim. And the land had rest for forty years.' (KJV)*

This account helps us to realise that when Israel cried unto the Lord, the spirit of the Lord came upon Othenial and he judged

Israel and went to war against the Mesopotamian king, and the Lord delivered him into his hands. There is victory over the enemy through the t quickening of the spirit. How many times as believer do we try to fight the battle ourselves and fall flat on our faces? Our victory will come if we let the spirit lead us.

Let's hear what a pagan king has to say about the Spirit of God. In Genesis 41:38 it reads, *'And Pharaoh said to his servants can we find such one as this is, a man in whom the Spirit of God is?'*

Here we come across an instance where a pagan king declares that Joseph has the Spirit of God upon him. Why? What did Pharaoh See and hear about Joseph? He saw a godly lifestyle, was also inpressed by the way he interpreted dreams supernaturally. Joseph was sold by his own brothers to people of a strange language in a strange land. This was a world of strange culture and ideals to people who knew no God and had no regard for God, a country whose king and inhabitants served other gods. He was a young man with no relative or friends he could relate to in a foreign land. Joseph did not run after the pleasures of Egypt, neither was he after the persuasive words of men wisdom, but he ran after God. He had no identity among the people he had been sold to, as a slave, but had God as his identity. He allowed himself for the Spirit of God to indwell for God's glory. Though a slave and also a stranger, he lived for God. With the spirit of God on him, he became different from the rest of the citizen in the way he lived and explain things. I tell you he had the wisdom and the knowledge of God, because he had the Spirit of God. Joseph by himself couldn't have interpreted Pharaoh's dream had not the Spirit of God been upon him.

How many times do we as Christians turn to rely on our own strength, thinking we can make it with no help? How often do we leave God behind instead of letting him lead us in every situation of our life? The dreams of Joseph came to pass when he became obedient to his God and his word. He had victory in all areas of his life, including the prosperity of his family. Please remember that where God leads, he surely provides and empowers

In particular, gifts of wisdom and discernment are given by the Spirit of God, which is declared the book of Deuteronomy 34:8-9: *'And, the children of Israel wept for Moses in the Plains of Moab thirty days so the days of weeping and morning for Moses were ended. And Joshua the son of Nun was full of the Spirit of wisdom for Moses had laid his hands on him, and the children of Israel hearkened unto him, and did as the Lord commanded Moses.'*

This record of Joshua being full of the spirit of wisdom, because Moses, his successor, had laid his hands on him, is deeper than we may think. For Israel to obey someone apart from the Prophet Moses, to lead them to the Promise Land was something Israel never dreamt, would ever happen to them. Moses is the only man of God who spoke face to face with him. He was the miracle man of God, the deliverer, the provider of food and water, the only one with the promise of God, to deliver Israel to the Promised Land that was flowing with milk and honey. A man who was not comparable to anyone. To Israel, Moses was their saviour. He is the one in all, with signs and wonders following him everywhere he went in the land of Egypt. He was mighty and full of terror to Pharaoh, to Egypt, and to the whole of Israel. To Pharaoh, God made him a god. There was not a prophet who arose in Israel like him, until we study his successor, when the spirit of God came upon him.

Joshua 1:1-6 says,

*Now after the death of Moses the servant of the Lord, it came to pass, that the Lord spoke unto Joshua the son of Nun, Moses minister, saying, Moses my servant is dead, now therefore arise, go over this Jordan, thou and all this people, unto the land which I do give to them, even to the children of Israel. Every place that the sole of your foot shall tread upon, that have I given unto you, as I said unto Moses. From the wildness and this Lebanon even unto the river, the river Euphrates, all the land of the Hittites, and unto the great sea toward the going down of the sun, shall be your coast. There shall not any man be able to stand before thee all the days of thy life, as I was with Moses so I will be with thee, I will not fail thee, nor forsake thee. Be strong and of a good courage, for unto this people shall thou divide for an inheritance the land which I swore unto their father to give them. (KJV)*

There is no success without a successor. Joshua, being his minister, was chosen by God to succeed Moses. Moses, representing the law, was already dead and Joshua (meaning Jehovah-saviour) was ordered by God and permitted to do what Moses could not do, namely, lead Israel to the promised land. Just as Christ was made under the law, but operated faithfully, and is able to lead us to his kingdom. So also did Joshua operated, so the promise for the Children of Israel can come to pass. Here, however, Joshua as the appointed leader, who knows the plan of the Lord for his people, needed to be incited to prompt action, and the people needed to be encouraged by the renewal of the divine command. God, therefore, needed to speak to the man who his spirit was upon to incite the people to action. During this time Israel thought they had suffered defeat because of the death of the Moses, the man of God. All the hope of Israel was gone. Having come that far and so close to the promised land, the River Jordan just in front of them with no deliverer, it was better for them to die than to live. In the midst of their weeping murmuring, complaining and waiting due to the death of Moses, God spoke to Joshua, the man who had his spirit of wisdom. God reminded and reaffirmed his covenant promise to the people of Israel, and that he would bring them to the promised land through the man he had chosen. God promised Israel he would bring them to their inheritance, and to Joshua he promised there shall be no man that would be able to stand before him all the days of his life, and that as he was with Moses, so he would be with him.

As we continue to study the scriptures, we come to realise that all the promises of God to Israel and Joshua came to pass. Israel got to the promised land and none was able to stand before Joshua. He led Israel to cross the River Jordan and achieved more and exceedingly. The man with the spirit of wisdom in his life fought many battles and won many. Where God lead, he brings promises to pass.

It is easy to get discouraged when a person you love and depend on dies, like a mother or a father, a brother or a sister, a doctor or an uncle on whom you solely depend. In such situations all hope will be gone. You may sometimes think there is no one to take the place of the person that you have lost. In these instances many give up, get depressed, become discourage, weep, murmur, and complain, like the people of Israel.

Remember that God is the captain of your salvation, not man. Man can promise you an oath and still fail you, but when God's promises it is certain. God never turned his back on the people of his covenant. He will always lead us to victory by his spirit. It is just as he spoke to Zerubbabel.

Zechariah 4:6 says, *'Then he answered and spoke unto me, saying, this is the word of the Lord unto Zerubbabe,l saying, not by might, nor by power, but by my spirit, said the Lord of hosts. '(KJV).* It is only the spirit that can energise us to walk in victory, and take the land. The promise of God to us can only come to pass if we work with God. This can only happen if we allow the Spirit of God to indwell in us. With the spirit upon Joshua's life, he was able to lead Israel to the promised land. My dear reader, it is not proper to talk about the spirit in individual life without writing about the work of the Holy Spirit in the life of Israel as a whole, which we shall do in the next chapter.

# CHAPTER 6

## *Where He Leads, He Directs*

Many at times we look to Israel and we begin to ask ourselves, why only Israel? Does God show partiality? Is he not a respecter of persons? Why did God deal with Israel more differently than any other nation on earth? What was exceptional about them? Why Israel and not, say, Britain or India? Is he the God of the children of Israel only or the God of the whole world?

We can ask ourselves these and many more questions, but I can assure you that they all come with answers and purposes in themselves. Israel was chosen as a priesthood nation to stand in the gap between man and God, bringing God to man and man to God. This was something that God in his future plans had in mind for those who would come and make Christ as their personal saviour and Lord. Israel was an example of God's plan for mankind. Just as believers are strangers and pilgrims, so also was Israel. Israel's position as a kingdom of priests and a holy nation did not come by chance or out the blue. It came with a condition. The condition was that if they obeyed the voice of the Lord and his covenant, then they should be a peculiar treasure unto him above all people. God declared 'that all the earth is mine'. Pass the test and win the crown. They were given the conditions, and if at any time they fulfilled the conditions, the promises came to pass. All Christians, wheresoever they may be, compose one holy nation.

They are one nation collected under one head, which is Christ Jesus our Lord, agreeing upon the same manner and customs and governed by the same laws, and they are a holy nation consecrated and devoted to God, renewed and sanctified by the Holy Spirit. Like Israel, Christians are a chosen generation, a royal priesthood, a peculiar people, not by chance, but with a condition. They should show forth the praises of him who has called them out of darkness into his marvellous light. The choice is yours. You may choose to be part of the Kingdom of light or part of the kingdom of darkness. The choice you make will determine who you are. God shows no partiality or favouritism, but those who respond to the conditions laid down will always see his blessing coming to pass in their lives. Let's sit back and look at a time in history when God gave a specific instruction to Moses, with regard to his sanctuary.

Exodus 25:1-9 says,

*"Then the Lord spoke to Moses, saying: 'speak to the children of Israel, that they bring me an offering. From everyone who gives it willing with his heart you shall take my offering. And this the offering which you shall take from them; gold, silver, bronze, blue and purple and scarlet yarn, fine linen thread, and goat hair, ram skin dyed red, badger skins, and acacia wood; oil for the light, and spices for the anointing oil and for the sweet incense, onyx stones, and stones to be set in the ephod and in the breastplate. And let them make me, a sanctuary that I may dwell among them. According to all that I show you that is the pattern of the tabernacle and the pattern of all its furnishings, just so you shall make it. (NKJV)*

The Lord commanded Moses, his servant, to build him a sanctuary. A tabernacle was a moveable tent that would be suitable for Israel's nomadic life. It was a dwelling place of God among his people, a place where the tables of the law, or testimony, could be kept, a place which the glory of the Lord would fill, and his presence there would lead the children of Israel on their journey. God had always promised his people he would not leave them or forsake them. He promised to remain in the midst of his people at all times. For Israel to apprehend this, God had to make his dwelling among them. By this I mean his visible presence, where consultation could be made at any time, wherever and whenever necessary.

With this in mind, God instructed Moses to tell the children of Israel to bring an offering willingly, to make him a sanctuary so that he might dwell among them. Remember, if you are going to give to God it has to be from a willing heart. Since the building of the Tabernacle was not like any ordinary house or building but a house of God, it had to be built by the direction of God himself. For this to happen, the Bible says the Lord filled the builders with the Spirit of God in wisdom and understanding.

Exodus 31:1-6 says,

*"Then the Lord spoke to Moses, saying, see, I have called by name Bezaleel the son of Uri, the son of Hur, of the tribe of Judah. And I have filled him with the Spirit of God, in wisdom, in understanding, in knowledge, and in all manner of workmanship, to design artistic works, to work in gold, in silver, in bronze, in cutting jewels for setting, in carving wood, and to work in all manner of workmanship. And I, indeed I, have appointed with him Aholiab the son of Ahisamach, of the tribe of Dan, and I have put wisdom in the heart of all who are gifted artisans, that they may make all that I have commanded you" (NKJV).*

God, in his own way, has plan and purpose for his people. Nothing on the face of the earth escapes the direction of God. As the songwriter wrote, he's got the whole world in his hands. History is *His story*. The house of the Lord needs to be built to his specifications. Nothing can be taken for granted in God's

requirement, just the same way God takes every individual believer into account of his plan and purpose. Even the hairs on our head are numbered. He knows us by name and has engraved us in the palms of his hands. God knows our flame. This indicates to all of us that every word of God will have its fulfilment. Nothing escapes the mighty hand of God. God is surely in control. When God calls he equips and directs. God equipped the builders in his service.

For Bezaleel of the tribe of Judah to be constructed the sanctuary of God, the Lord filled him with the spirit of God in wisdom and understanding in all manner of workmanship, so as to enable him to carry on the work of God. This proves to all Christians that we cannot underestimate the power of the Holy Spirit in the daily life of the individual believer. Are you called to do the work of the ministry? Then don't sit back and think you can make it happen without the power of the spirit. Don't forget what happened to the apostles after the death of the Lord Jesus; they still haven't received the promise of the Holy Spirit. The scriptures declare that they all went back to fishing. They couldn't do the work of the ministry without the power of the Holy Spirit. It is the spirit who influences us to do the work of God, to his specifications. The spirit is the breath of the power of God that influences the glory of the Almighty. It is also the spirit who makes friends of God and prophets. The Spirit of God causes us to gain knowledge of the counsel of God. The gift of prophecy comes as a result of the spirit's presence upon us.

It can be strange sometimes, but eclectic powers induced suddenly in certain ways in the Old Testament times, as the spirit came upon men and women to prophecy. The spirit caused the men of old not only to prophecy but also to interpret dreams, as the spirit came upon them, as it was in the life of Daniel in the Babylonian Empire as a slave in the king's palace.

Daniel 4:8 says, '*At last Daniel came in before me, he who was named Belteshazzar after the name of my god, in whom is the spirit of the spirit of Holy gods, and I told him the dream saying.*'

This was the time of Babylonian history when Nebuchadnezzar, King of Babylon, had a dream and troubling. He called all the magicians the astrologers, the Chaldeans, and the soothsayers of the land and demanded an interpretation of the vision, but he had no success. Remember, they were all carnally minded, and carnally minded people do not understand the things of God. But here we see that Daniel, who had the spirit of God upon him, came and gave the interpretation of the dream in a situation where there was no hope. This made king Nebuchadnezzar believe that Daniel's God was truly the God of all gods, the Lord of kings, and a revealer of secrets. He also made Daniel a great man and gave him many gifts and made him ruler over the whole province of Babylon and a chief of the governors over all the wise men of Babylon. Daniel lived life to the full, to a good old age, with the spirit of the Lord upon him. Not only did Daniel interpret dreams, but he had many revelations of the end time. Much of the hereafter of God was revealed to Daniel, much of which has been fulfilled and much of which has yet to be fulfilled. Where the Spirit of God is at work, there is always prophecy and revelations. Step out of the spirit's guidance and there is deception and no knowledge, and for lack of knowledge God's, people perish.

# CHAPTER 7

## *The Presence of God at Israel's Camp*

The love of God for his people is so great that he instructed Moses to build him a Tabernacle where his presence would dwell in their midst. With his presence in their midst they could present their case and reason together with him. Where his presence dwells he instructs, and where he instructs there is victory. With God's presence we can move from victory to victory, just as Israel enjoyed victory over all its enemies even as they depended on the direction of God who not only promised them but was also able to fulfil what he promised.

The holy of holies of the Tabernacle contained the awesome glory or presence of God. With the Ark of the Covenant, Israel enjoyed much victory. God instructed Joshua along these lines.

*And Joshua said unto the people, sanctify yourself for tomorrow the Lord will do wonders among you. And Joshua spoke unto the priest saying take up the Ark of the Covenant, and passes over before the people. And they took ups the Ark of the Covenant and went before the people. And the Lord said unto Joshua, this day will I begin to magnify thee in the sight of all Israel that they may know that, as I was with Moses, so I will be with thee. And thou shall command the priest that bears the ark of covenant, saying when you come to the brink of the water of Jordan; yea shall stand still in Jordan.*

*And Joshua said unto the children of Israel, come hither and hears the words of the Lord your God. And Joshua said, hereby you shall know that the living God is among you, and that he will without fail drive out from before you the Canaanites, and the Hittites and the Hivites and the Perizzites and the Girgashites and the Amorites and the Jebusites. Behold, the Ark of the Covenant of the Lord of all the earth passeth over before you into Jordan. Now therefore take your twelve men out of the tribes of Israel, out of every tribe a man. And it shall come to pass, as soon as the soles of the feet of the priest that bear the ark of the Lord, the Lord of all the earth, shall rest in the waters of the Jordan, that the waters of Jordan shall be cut off from the waters that come down from above, and they shall stand upon a heap.* (Joshua 3:5-13 KJV)

God planned to give Israel a breakthrough in their journey to the promised land. As Israel progress to the promised land, they found themselves at the banks of the river Jordan, just as Moses also found himself at the bank of the Red Sea. Spies viewed the land and came back with a good report, saying to Joshua, truly the Lord has delivered into our hands all the land, for even all the inhabitants of the country do faint because of us. The only hurdle in front of them at that point was the River Jordan. How was Israel going to cross with their sons and daughters, livestock and livelihood, to inherit their God-given promise? Just as they were contemplating how to get over, God assured Joshua that he was with them, just as he was with Moses. The plan of God for Israel was to bear the Ark of the Covenant and bring it to the midst of the Jordan, where their miracle would take place. The question is why the Ark of the Covenant; the answer is because it signifies the presence of God. With the ark leading the procession through the River Jordan, Israel had hope. They realised that God was leading them to their inheritance. When Israel sanctified them and became obedient to the instructions of God, they saw the glory of God in their lives. Not only did the Lord cause the River Jordan to stand upon a heap for Israel to cross, but he also drove out from before them the Canaanites, the Hittites, the Hivites, the Perizzites, the Girgashites, the Amorites, and the Jebusites. Where God leads, there he always give victory.

I would like you to remember that that whatever the promise of God for your life is, it will surely come to pass if you let him lead you. It is God who promised; therefore, allow him to bring it to pass. Remember, all the promises of God are in him, yes, and we are the one to say Amen to the glory of God the Father. Physically it was impossible for Israel to cross the river, but when they released their faith, they received from God. How? They did not allow the things they saw and heard in the natural world to intimidate them, but they allowed themselves to be led by the spirit.

The scriptures declares, *'But the natural man receive not the things of the spirit of God, for they are foolishness unto him, neither can he know them, because they are spiritually discerned'* (1 Cor 2:14).

We need to quit living in the natural realm and come to God's spiritual realm to be able to receive spiritual things. Begin to discern spiritual things of God by having the mind of Christ. Having the mind of Christ will enable you to live spirit-filled life.

*Now Jericho was strictly shut up because of the children of Israel, none went out, and none came in. and the Lord said unto Joshua, see I have given into thin hand Jericho, and the king thereof, and the mighty men of valour. And ye shall compass the city, all ye men of war, and go round the city once. Thus shalt thou do six days? And seven priests shall bear before the ark seven trumpets of rams' horns, and the seventh day ye shall compass the city seven times, and the priests shall blow with the trumpets. And it shall come to pass, that when they make a long blast with the ram's horn, and when ye hear the sound of the trumpet, all the people shall shout with a great shout, and the wall of the city shall fall down flat, and the people shall ascend up every man straight before him.* (Joshua 6:1-5 NKJV)

This is a very important scenario that Israel found itself in, indicating what the presence of God can do in the lives of his people. God always brings his people to a place where they can depend on him. You can see for yourself what happens to those who depend on God to bring to pass their heart's desire. With the presence of God in the midst of Israel, the city of Jericho fell down flat and the king thereof and the mighty men of valour were placed in the hands of Israel. It wasn't by might or by power, but through their obedience to the word of God that came to them. Where the presence of God is, there will always be victory.

Joshua always went with the Ark of the Covenant, or testimony, and never lost a battle. But when men try to manipulate the spirit or the presence of God, there is always anarchy, and people are sometimes killed as a result.

A typical example is the case of Hophini and Phinehas, the two sons of Eli.

*And the word of Samuel came to all Israel. Now Israel went out against the Philistines to battle, and pitched beside Ebenezer, and the Philistines pitched in Aphek. And the Philistines put themselves in array against Israel, and when they joined battle, Israel was smitten before the Philistines, and they slaw of the army in the field about four thousand men. And when the people were coming into the camp, the elders of Israel said, wherefore hath the Lord smitten us today before the Philistines? Let us fetch the ark of the covenant of the Lord out of Shiloh unto us, that when it cometh among us, it may save us out of the hands of our enemies. So the people sent to Shiloh, that they might bring from thence the ark of the covenant of the Lord of hosts, which dwelled between the cherubim, and the two sons of Eli, Hophni and Phinehas, were there with the ark of the covenant of God. And when the ark of the covenant of the LORD came into the camp, all Israel shouted with a great shout, so that the earth rang again. And when the Philistines heard the noise of the shout, they said, What meanest the noise of this great shout in the camp of the Hebrews? And they understood that the ark of the LORD was come into camp. And the Philistines were afraid, for they said, Woe unto us! For there hath not been such a thing heretofore. Woe unto us! Who shall deliver us out of the hand of these mighty gods? These are the gods that smote the Egyptians with all the plagues in the wilderness. Be strong and quit yourselves like men, O ye Philistines, that ye be not servants unto the Hebrews, as they have been to you, quit yourselves like men and fight. And the Philistines fought, and Israel was smitten, and they fled every man into his tent, and there was a very great slaughter, for there fell of Israel thirty thousand footmen. And the ark of God was taken, and the two sons of Eli, Hophni and Phinehas, were slain.* (1 Samuel 4:1-11 KJV)

When the Philistines camped against Israel at Aphek and fought against, Israel was smitten, and about four thousand men of Israel's army were slain. Hophni and Phinehas thought it was a wise decision to bring the Ark of the Covenant to the camp of Israel, but when they did the Philistines became afraid. Why? Was it because they realised the power that was in the Ark? The Ark indicates power and victory to Israel. The tenth verse of the same chapter tells us the opposite of Israel conceptions. Instead of victory in the camp of Israel, they were smitten, and about thirty thousand Israelites were slaughtered.

Man cannot manipulate the power of God. When we become obedient to God and his word he will work with us to bring about the victory that we seek. It is his power that he gives to those who become obedient. You and I can never put God in a box, for he is an awesome God. His grace abounds more and more and his mercy endures forever. In obedience he will always grant us victory.

# CHAPTER 8

## *The Fullness of God in Christ*

I have been around for a while, but I still haven't come across any individual who has it all or knows it all. Yes, there are many specialists in various professions, people we sometime call genius. They still can't match the qualities and abilities of their maker. There is no way the creature can be compared to the creator. The scriptures say that the only individual who had all the qualities of God is Jesus.

John 10:10 says, *'The thief comes not, but for to steal and to kill, and to destroy, I am come that they might have life and that they might have it more abundantly.'* The devil wishes the downfall of all mankind. He brings people under his domain only to steal, kill, and destroy their life. But Jesus, the only one who had it all together, came that we might have life and then have it in abundance. Not only does he protect what belongs to us, but also he buys us back and restores all that we have lost.

Colossians 2:9 says, *'For in him dwelled all the fullness of the Godhead bodily. And you are complete in him, which is the head of all principality and power.'* The only way we can be complete is when our life is found in Christ. There are principality and power, but Christ can bring us to the place where we are able to overcome these elements. Yes, there can be obstacles in the way of our success and prosperity, but in Christ we are more than conquerors. The scripture cannot state more plainly that if God is for us no one can stand against us. Let us look at it this way. How many men and women together can ever equate God, the creator? We need to remember that all creation together can never equate the creator. That's why we as humans need to realise the important work of our Lord and saviour Jesus on the cross at Calvary. This proves that he can stand and atone for all mankind as a man whilst at the same time remaining God. The devil has no right over us, for he does not belong here. He operates here illegally. He was not born here; neither did he inherit flesh and blood. He assumes authority by deception and intimidation. But thank God for his revelation to all mankind through the Lord Jesus. How did this happen?

Galatians 4:5 says, '*But when the fullness of the time had come God sent forth his Son, born of a woman, born under the law, to redeem those who were under the law, that we might receive the adoption as sons.*' God through his grace and mercy fulfilled his promise to Abraham, by sending his son to redeem them that were under the law. He was actually born here and therefore has authority here as well. In his sinless state he became sin that the righteousness of God would be imputed upon us. Christ is our rightful representation and our rightful owner.

Galatians 3:8-9 says, '*And the scripture, foreseeing that God would justify the Gentiles by faith, preached the gospel to Abraham beforehand, saying, In you all the nation shall be blessed. So then those who are of faith are blessed with believing Abraham.*' When he promises he always delivers. God foreknew the state of man and therefore promised deliverance even before it happened. Who said God was not in control? No matter who you are, you fall under the perfect plan of God.

It is sometime bothering when we pick up the Bible and read the way God dealt with certain characters, and also the various rituals that we read about. Without proper understanding it becomes very difficult and confusing. Why all these rituals and festivals? Are they really for the believer of today? Many have concluded that the Old Testament is not for today's Christian. I do strongly disagree with people who hold such views. We need to understand that, the New Testament has not much clarity until we came to understand the Old Testament. I see the New Testament as the fulfilment of the promises in the Old Testament. Whilst the Old Testament messages are types and shadows of the things to comes, the New Testament is the fulfilment of the things to come. Yes, not all the prophecies have been fulfilled; there are yet some prophecies to be fulfilled. Just as the New Testament has great value, so also does the Old Testament.

We need to realise that all scripture is inspired by God. But before we can appreciate the Old Testament, we need to understand the purpose for which it was written. For instance, we cannot take the Ten Commandments for granted, since this is the way God introduced himself to Israel, as a Holy God and man sinful. In addition to the commandments God gave Israel special instruction for the building of a Tabernacle, which we discussed in the previous chapter. It was an elaborate system of worship, sacrifices, and ordaining of priesthood. In order for man to come to God, he needs to come to the Tabernacle where the presence God was. This is the ordained way of God to get to him. God is Holy and man is sinful, and that without holiness, no one can see God.

For man to come to God he needs to come through the Tabernacle, not empty-handed but with blood. God never intended Israel to come to him by trying to keep the Ten Commandments. The Ten Commandments cannot offer the blood evidence of a life given. Exodus 24:8 indicates that the blood confirms and seals the covenant the Lord made with Israel in giving them the law.

God intended for men to come to him through the way he provided. That is by blood, through the Tabernacle. Through the blood there would be forgiveness of sin. This approach was by blood administered by the priest and at God's Tabernacle, where the presence of God dwells. By blood through the Tabernacle was the only way to come to God, and every other way was not accepted.

Leviticus 17:11 says, *'For the life of the flesh is in the blood, and I have given it to you upon the altar to make atonement for your souls'*; for it is the blood that makes atonement for the soul. The only way we can understand the finished work of our saviour Jesus is to understand the setup, the sacrifice, the priesthood, and the organisation of the Tabernacle as a whole. The construction, the furniture, the equipment, and their functions all point to Christ who was to come. It all pointed to the promised Messiah of God to Moses. It points to the seed that God promised Abraham. Our total understanding of the Old and the New Testament would come when we began to understand the entire elaborate system, piece by piece, and put them together. The Old Testament on its own is incomplete, as is the New on its own. The two testaments together, therefore, constitute the perfect plan of God for mankind as a whole.

Let us for a moment look at the Jewish Tabernacle and its courtyard. The courtyard was about half the size of a football field, with the Tabernacle in the middle. Only the priest could go to the inside the Tabernacle, but the high priest could go to the inner chamber, called the Holy of Holies. This can be done only once a year, and always with blood, the only thing that can make atonement for the soul.

John 1:14 says, *'And the word became flesh and dwelt among us, and we beheld his glory, the glory as of the only begotten of the Father, full of grace and truth.'* In the Greek language the word 'skenoo' means *tabernacle, or to patch a tent or to dwell.* Christ, being the image of the in visible God, became flesh and dwelt among men.

God in the Old Testament dwelt in the Tabernacle, but in the New Testament he dwelt in the flesh, among men, as Christ. Paul in the book of Galatians puts it very simply. *'But when the fullness of the time had come, God sent forth His Son, born of a woman, born under the law'* (Galatians 4:4). The Tabernacle of old was in the new the body of Christ. On the day of Pentecost He sent forth hi spirit to dwell in man. This is what is know as the Holy Spirit baptism which believers receive when they make the Lord Jesus their lord and personal saviour. The glory of God had dwelt in the Holy of Holies, in the earthly Tabernacle and temple made with hands. Now it was to dwell in the man Jesus, the Heavenly Tabernacle made without hands Now in Christ Jesus you and I have been sealed with the Holy Spirit which is the Father's promise.

The covering of the Tabernacle was also fascinating. The outer covering of the Tabernacle was made of badger's skin—unattractive and dull in colour. This reminds me of what Nathaniel said to Philip in John 1:45-46a: *'Philip found Nathaniel and said to him. We have found him of whom Moses in the law, and also the prophets, wrote Jesus of Nazareth, the son of Joseph. And Nathaniel said to him, "Can anything good come from Nazareth?"'* Jesus on the outside was nobody. On the outside he was just the carpenter's son. He was just like any ordinary man. But on the inside he was like the Tabernacle's red-dyed ram skin—the glory and the divine nature of God runs through his veins. Like the badger's skin, God's glory in the Tabernacle was veiled in Jesus, the carpenter, to the onlookers. But through his shared blood upon the Calvary cross, the glory of God is revealed. Just like Jesus before, he was glorified, the Christian has no value, outside Christ, until they come to the revelation knowledge of God. Until we come to know God and the power of his resurrection, we will never appreciate the work of God in our lives.

When standing outside the only way into the Tabernacle is through the gate. The gate is the entrance to the eastern side of the Tabernacle. The tribe of Judah had their camp by the eastern gate, with a gold lion upon a scarlet background as their banner. There is so much we can learn from these combinations. Jesus was from the tribe of Judah. Gold represents deity. A lion denote a king or ruler as the symbol of the tribe of Judah. This shows how Jesus the Christ fulfilled this role as a king who descended the from the throne of David. John on the island of Patmos saw Jesus as the lion of Judah (Revelation 5:5). The Scarlet field can be said to represent the blood shared at a battlefield. Not to mention Jesus, the only Son of God, shared his blood at the Calvary cross. Ezekiel 43:4 says, *'And the glory of the Lord came into the house by the way of gate whose prospect is towards the east.'* Christ himself said, *'I am the way the truth and the life.'* Does this prove he is the gate of the Tabernacle? Christ is the only one who fulfilled this role.

John 10:10 says, 'The thief does not come except to steal, and to kill, and to destroy, I have come that they may have life, and that they may have it more abundantly.' This proves to us the work of the devil in our life. There is no good that comes from him. The only one who can give us life, and an abundant life, is Christ Jesus. How did he do that? The next furniture of the Tabernacle helps us to understand it very well. He is not only the gate to the Tabernacle but also the brazen altar. Leviticus 17:11 states, *'For the life of the flesh is in the blood, and I have given it to you upon the altar to make atonement for your souls, for it is the blood that makes atonement for the souls.'* (NKJV)

The New Testament makes it clear that Christ became our sacrificial lamb. No matter how morally sound you may be in

Israel, you need to come to God with the sacrifice of blood. You cannot come to God though the law or the Ten Commandments, for no one was able to follow the law perfectly. It is only through the blood sacrificed on the altar in the Tabernacle. One can choose to kill so many lambs and cows or goats outside the camp of the Tabernacle as they want, but the blood will serve no purpose. Until we offer our sacrifice as stipulated by God, it will not be accepted. Our obedience to God makes the difference. Anything less doesn't matter. In the New Testament the cross became the altar upon which Christ, our sacrificial lamb, was offered for the forgiveness of sins. The blood of the lamb was poured at the base of the altar, just like the blood of Jesus at the foot of the cross at Calvary where Jesus died. Luke makes it clear that, at the revelation of Jesus to his disciples after the resurrection, there was no blood left in him, for he was made of flesh and bone. All his blood was shed at the foot of the cross; just as the blood of the lamb at the camp of Israel serves as atonement for sin, so also does the blood of Jesus.

Paul explained it in the book of Romans 3:23: *that 'for allhave sin and have fall short of the glory of God'. The writer of the book of Hebrew also reminds us that, 'without the shedding of blood there is no forgiveness of sin.'* It is therefore the blood that brings us to God, not works of righteousness. Our righteousness, the scripture says, is like filthy rags; how then can we please God with it? We need to be thankful to God who has given us Christ as our sin substitute. In Christ we have become the righteousness of God. This was done through his bloodshed on the cross at Calvary.

A piece of furniture that stairs at you before you enter the Tabernacle is a brazen lever. This was a washing basin made of polish brass that can also be used as a mirror. This was also the basin in which Aaron's sons were washed when they were consecrated. This basin was where the priest saw himself dirty, and therefore needed to be cleansed by its water. What does this cleansing indicate in the life of unbeliever? Unless we are born of water and of the spirit, we cannot enter the Kingdom of God. Jesus gave himself to be baptised.

Peter in his sermon to the Jews in Jerusalem said to them, 'Repent, and let everyone of you be baptised in the name of Jesus Christ for the remission of sins and you shall receive the gift of the Holy Spirit.' The brazen lever (a mirror like object) points the priest to the fact that he is dirty and needs to wash. James 1:23-25 says, *'For if anyone is a hearer of the word and not a doer, he is like a man observing his natural face in the mirror. For he observes and he, goes away, and immediately forgets what kind of man he was. But he who look into the perfect law of liberty and continues in it and is not a forgetful hearer but a doer of the word this one will be blessed in what he does.'* The word of God is our mirror. In the word we see how sinful we are and how we can be saved. It shows how we by ourselves cannot make it, until we look unto him. We need both the washing of water and of the spirit to be able to enter the Kingdom of God, just as without washing the priest cannot enter the holy place.

The holy place contains three pieces of furniture, all of which have their significance. The first object of furniture is the golden candlestick, which stands on the left-hand side of the room. It is the only light in the room. It has seven branches, with the middle branch supplying the oil to the other six branches. Oil is a symbol of Holy Spirit. 1 John 1:5 says, *'God is light.'* John 9:5 says, *'I am the light of the world'*; this is Jesus talking about himself. Also referring to his disciples he said, 'You are the light of the world.' The whole golden candlestick represents God himself. The stem is Christ, and the branches are we, the believers. Gold represents deity. The only light in this world today is that of the believers. Take them away and the world would be full of darkness. We will fall flat on our faces if we try to do it by ourselves. It is only when the Holy Spirit shines in our lives that we can in turn illuminate the world. He is our source of power.

The next bit of furniture in the Holy place is the table of showbread; this table holds twelve loaves of bread and a cup of wine. Each loaf represents a tribe of Israel, the priesthood nation made to stand in the gap between God and man. This represents the blood covenant meal, pointing to the time when man would have communion with God through the Holy Spirit. The breaking of the bread helps us remember his death in our place and his coming again for those who wait for his appearing. When the Lord shared the Passover meal with his disciples, He indicated to them that the bread was his body and the wine was his blood which was sooner or later going to be shed for all men so that their sins may be forgiven.

There was a time with his disciples when he said his blood would be shed for all men and his body broken for them. This means that unless they ate his flesh and drank his blood, they would have no life. He is the bread that came down from heaven. This made many of his disciples desert him. He then turned to the twelve and asked if they would also go away, but Simon Peter said, "Lord, to whom shall we go? You have the words of eternal life." To have life we need to come to the giver of life. He said I have come that you might have life and have it in abundance. We spend time on what is not food, and labour on things that do not satisfy. The only thing that can satisfy is the bread of heaven. We need to come and buy the bread and wine that comes from above with no money and at no cost. The word of God is that which satisfies. It is the spirit that quickens the flesh and profits nothing; it is the word that is spirit and life. For your life in abundance began to dive into the word of God.

The altar of incense is the third artefact in the holy place. This is the place where incense is offered morning and evening on burning coals. On the Day of Atonement, which is the tenth of October, the priest will sprinkle blood from the brazen altar on the altar of incense. Incense is a symbol of prayer. With the incense on the coals of fire, the smoke will surge and bulge up in front of the priest, as he enters the Holy of Holies. This gives the priest access to the presence of God to offer the prayer of the people. Jesus, just before he was offered for our sin offering, he prayed the high priestly prayer for those of us who will come to believe in his name.

Jesus is worthy to intercede on our behalf, because it was his own blood that was sprinkle on the horn of the altar at the cross of Calvary. Through the shedding of his blood, God has highly exalted Christ and has given him a name that is above all named. At the name all knees shall bow and every tongue shall confess that Jesus is Lord. With his blood, Christ was able to enter the holy of Holies without the Vail. It was the Vail that hides the glory of God from the public. Mark recorded that when Jesus gave up his ghost, the Vail of the temple was rent in twain from top to bottom, signifying a new access to the presence God. The broken Vail allows us to get to the presence of God. Not only the Jews but also the gentiles have access to God through Christ.

Our final destination is to the Holy of Holies, where the presence of God is. This is where the 'skenoo' glory, or the dwelling of God, was. This is the place where God promises to reveal his visible presence to his people. It was this glorious cloud that hid Israel from the pursuing Egyptians. It also lighted the way of the Israelis at night through the wilderness, and it became darkness to the Egyptians. It was this glory that covered the mountain Sinai. It is the same cloud of glory that overshadowed them on the mountain of transfiguration. When Christ was taken up to the heavens it was this cloud that received him out of their sight. The only artefact in the Holy of Holies was the Ark of Covenant. The lid attached to the Ark is known as the mercy seat. This place is called Holy of Holies because no unclean person can enter and come back. For this reason the high priest has to cleanse him before entering the Holy of Holies. He also has to wear robe with bells hanging on it and with a long rope tied to his waist. The bell will raise the alarm in case of any eventualities, and the long rope will help to pull him out of the room.

The Holy of Holies is the place where the blood is applied to cover the sins of Israel, but once and for all Christ became the propitiation for our sins. Not like the high priest, who has to enter the Holy of Holies once in a year to plead for the sins of his people of Israel to be covered, but once and for all Christ, with his own blood. He applied his blood to the mercy seat to cover the sins of all mankind. Christ became our high priest after the order of Melchizedek. With his blood he turned away the wrath of God away from guilty sinners by enduring the wrath of God himself on the cross at Calvary.

Paul wrote in the book of Romans that '*the wrath of God is revealed from heaven against all ungodliness and unrighteousness of men*'. Man has sin, and because of that he needs to be saved. The only way to turn God's wrath is through blood offering. In book of Leviticus 17:11 we read, '*The life of the flesh is in the blood, and I have it to you upon the altar to make an atonement for your souls, for it is the blood that makes an atonement for the soul.*' Man's sins need to be atoned for, but not with the blood of bulls and goats, which only cover the sins for a year, but with the precious blood of Christ, which is able to take away all our sins. The blood of Jesus opens the way for all to go right into the presence of God and commune with God through the Holy Spirit. Jesus as the perfect sacrifice ascended into the heavenly Holy of Holies to sprinkle his own blood on the mercy seat in the heavenly throne room and then sat on it.

In Paul's letter to the Colossians, he said, '*In Christ we have redemption through his blood, even the forgiveness of sins.*' There is nothing more that we can do except what Christ has already done. With faith in the finished work of Christ, we gain access to his presence, where there is grace. In his presence there is fullness of joy. In his presence we receive our joy and our direction.

# CHAPTER 9

## *The Power of the Holy Spirit in the Church*

The expansion of the church came as a result of the outpouring of the Holy Spirit on the eyewitnesses of the resurrection and fellow believers. Jesus' promise to the disciples was that they would receive power when the Holy Spirit came upon them, and they would be his witness in Jerusalem and in all Judea and in Samaria, and in the outermost part of the world. This promise was fulfilled in the day of Pentecost. This also renewed their hope, which was in the prophecy of Joel.

Joel 2:28-29 states, *'And it shall come to pass afterward, that I will pour out my Spirit upon all flesh, and your sons and your daughters shall prophesy, your old men shall dream dreams, your young men shall see visions; And also upon the servants and upon the handmaids in those days will pour out my Spirit.'*

This prophecy came to fulfilment on the day of Pentecost, in the early Church. Acts 2:1-4 says, *'And when the day of Pentecost was fully come, they were all with one accord in one place. And suddenly there came a sound from heaven as of a rushing mighty winds, and filled all the house where they were sitting. And there appeared unto them cloven tongues like as of fire, and it sat upon each of them. And they were all filled with the Holy Ghost, and began to speak with other tongues, as the Spirit gave utterance.' (KJV)*

The disciples of the Lord Jesus went back to their own business after his death. Most of them to fishing and minding their own business, but they soon remembered what the Lord commanded them to do, '*not to depart from Jerusalem, but to wait for the promise of the father, which, saith he, ye have heard of me*'. Calling to mind this promise, the hundred and twenty people came together in the upper room to await God's next move. The promise was therefore received on the day of Pentecost, as described above, and made them able witnesses. All the recipients became infected as the spirit rested on them. Not only were they able to speak in other tongues, but they also received the power to declare the word of God with all boldness. This power so great that as the disciples opened their mouths to speak, many believed, and at one time three thousand people were saved. Many supernatural signs did follow the recipients as the Lord worked miracles through their hands.

It is the Holy Spirit that helps men to come to the revelation knowledge of Jesus. The coming down of the Holy Spirit in the day of Pentecost marked the constitution of the Church in history. It also marked the growth and expansion of the Church, not only in Jerusalem but also in the world as a whole. The fulfilment of this prophecy brought about life that was marked with unity. Believers that were added to the Church also received the power of the Holy Ghost, just as the disciples did. They had things in common through contributions and sharing of wealth as they were led. With the spirit as the common denominator, their needs were supplied, and none of them did lack anything; neither was there any needy person among them. With much power did the disciples continue to testify to the resurrection of the Lord Jesus, and much grace was upon them. Not only did they speak the word with all boldness, but they also instituted the breaking of bread, and prayer was born and enforced in the Church. The unity brought about by the spirit enabled them to come together. Daily they came together to share the work of the Lord, pray, and worship in the temple. The coming of the spirit brought not only power but also an outstanding community, with joy born into it. The favour of God was upon the new movement, which was the congregation of believers, who had an overwhelming experience.

How often do believers take for granted the spirit power in the work that God has called us to do? Pentecost was the occasion when the whole body of the disciples had the experience of the risen power of Jesus, which made Peter and the twelve new men. It also took the Holy Spirit to bring life to the church, which is still alive today. Who said we could make it without the spirit quickening? The gentile Pentecost in the house of Cornelius is also marked by the Holy Ghost power and the speaking of tongues, a pattern doubtless often repeated when the gospel message is preached and received.

## THE POWER OF GOD IN A BELIEVER'S TRIALS

The beginning of the Church, according to Luke, is marked by the constant presence of the Holy Spirit as supernatural power. When the apostles were persecuted for healing the poor lame man at the gate called Beautiful, this is what Peter said when he stood in the midst of the people, filled with the Holy Spirit. *'Rulers and the elders of the people, if we are being called to give accounts today for an acts of kindness shown to a cripple and are asked how he was healed, then know this, it is by the name of Jesus Christ of Nazareth whom you crucified but whom God raised from the dead, that this man stand before you healed.'* This was said with such boldness that it touched the heart and minds of the people, and many believed.

Stephen also experiences the power in his life, which went about in the grace of God with signs and wonders following. You may ask why he was so full of power. It is because he was full of faith and Holy Spirit. So also were many signs and wonders that accompanied the gift of the Spirit at Antioch.

The word records that Agabus stood up and through the spirit predicted that severer famine would spread over the entire Roman world; this happen during the reign of Claudius. We need to realise that the Spirit of God operates differently in each man's life. The Spirit does not always come just like the day of Pentecost., but also through the laying on of hands the spirit was bestowed on the believers. The spirit brought much accomplishment to many in the early Church and the Church of today. The spirit is for all believers and is not a private possession. The baptism of the Holy Spirit transforms the Christian believer's way of operating in the things of God. The spirit brought a society that was full of love, joy, and hope.

The Church outside Pentecost is dead, but the society of believers with the presence of the spirit of God is worth joining. If we don't understand the work of the Holy Spirit for believers and the Church as a whole, then we need to pray for God's directions and stop saying that it is the work of the devil. If all good and perfect things come from above, why would God give me the devil when I pray for the Holy Spirit? If believers let the Holy Spirit dwell in us to the full, then we will not even need to defend ourselves when we face trials and difficulties. He is meant to be our helper, but he will help only if we ask him.

## THE WORK OF THE HOLY SPIRIT IN MAN'S SALVATION

Acts 2:37-39 says, *'Now when they heard this, they were pricked in their heart, and said unto Peter and to the rest of the apostles, Men and brethren, what shall we do? Then Peter said unto them, Repent, and be baptised every one of you in the name of Jesus Christ for the remission of sins, and ye shall receive the gift of the Holy Ghost. For the promise is unto you, and to your children, and to all that are afar off, even as many as the Lord our God shall call.'* When Peter and the apostles received the Holy Ghost, they were quick to declare the word of God with all boldness. In their preaching, many believed and were pricked in their hearts and demanded from them, 'What should we do to receive salvation?' He requested they repent and be baptised.

It takes true repentance, baptism by immersion, and the indwelling of the Holy Spirit to bring about true salvation to the believer. Until we identify with the Lord Jesus, we will be fighting a losing battle.

The believer should realise that he has sinned, and the wages of sin is death. In this position we cannot save ourselves, and therefore we need to repent of our sins and our iniquities, which brought separation between us and our God. Our repentance should be that of the heart. The scriptures say with the heart man believes unto righteousness, and with the mouth confession is made unto salvation. Godly sorrows are the motivating factor of true repentance. Just as the people of Nineveh repented of their sins when the world of the Lord form the mouth of Jonah came to them, so do we need to repent. The only element that brings joy in the presence of the angels of God is the one sinner who repents. If you were that individual who is still living in sin, then I would ask you to bring joy to the angels of God with your repentance.

Our baptism serves as identification with the Lord Jesus. Paul, in his writing to the Romans, said, *'As many of us were baptised into Jesus Christ were baptised into his death.'* His death becomes our death. It is the death that we were supposes to die, because of our life. In Galatians 3:27, Paul said, *'For as many of you as have been baptised into Christ have put on Christ.'* We put on Christ when we are baptised, and we become new creation as a result. Our baptism is an act that the Lord himself commanded the Church.

Peter encouraged believers that repentance and baptism in the name of Jesus Christ would result in the remission of sins and the receiving of the Holy Ghost. We need the Holy Spirit to be able to have that supernatural walk with our Lord and saviour. In obedience God will pour out the gift of the Holy Spirit on us, just as he did in the lives of the disciples. Remember the biblical evidence of the Holy Spirit's power in the believer's life—the speaking of other tongues. Just as in Matthew, speaking in tongues is a sign that follow believers. We must be baptised not only in water but also in the spirit.

Let's for a moment share what the Lord Jesus said to Nicodemus, a ruler of the Jews. John 3:1-6 (KJV) states,

> *There was a man of the Pharisees, named Nicodemus, a ruler of the Jews: The same came to Jesus by night, and said unto him, Rabbi, we know that thou art a teacher come from God, for no man can do these miracles that thou doest, except God be with him. Jesus answered and said unto him, verily, verily, I say unto thee, Except a man be born again, he cannot see the kingdom of God. Nicodemus saith unto him, how can a man be born when he is old? Can he enter the second time into his mother's womb, and be born? Jesus answered, verily, verily, I say unto thee, Except a man is born of water and of the spirit he cannot enter into the kingdom of God. That which is born of the flesh is flesh; and that which is born of the Spirit is spirit.*

This was a very important question we believers need to take note of.

If we truly seek the Kingdom, then we need to know what it takes. This is why we must be baptised not only in water but also in the spirit. For our complete salvation we need to go through these three ordained steps: repentance, baptism, and the infilling of the Holy Ghost. We need to bear in mind that flesh gives birth to flesh, and spirit also gives birth to spirit.

## THE MAN WITH THE SPIRIT INDWELLING

Romans 8:1-2 states, *'There is therefore now no condemnation to them, which are in Christ Jesus, who walk not after the flesh, but after the Spirit. For the law of the Spirit life in Christ Jesus has made me free from the law of sin and death.'* Paul here was calling believers to mind the work of the spirit in the believer's life. He said those who walk after the spirit and not after the flesh have life in Christ Jesus, who set us free from the law of sin and death. Separation from sin comes about in the indwelling spirit. In verses 5 and 6, Paul says, 'For they that are after the flesh do mind the things of the flesh, but they that are after the Spirit, the things of the Spirit. For to be carnally minded is death; but to be spiritually minded is life and peace.' (KJV)

Believers needs to know how they walk, live, and move in the Kingdom. What are the things of this life that we mind? Are you that individual who focuses on the things of this world? Dependency on the provisions of this life leads to death. For life and peace, we need to mind the things of the spirit. Carnal-mindedness brings believers from grace to disgrace. *Sarkikos* is the Greek word for carnal, which means affinity to natural sinful propensities. The individual for whom the flesh is the ruling principle always lives in sin and death. Without the spirit indwelling and the word of

God, the individual cannot submit to the law of God. One who does not adhere to the word of God has no faith in himself to please God. The only cash available to believers to buy from the heavenly shops is our faith. This comes from hearing, and hearing by the word of God. How then do you get faith if your mind is not subjected to the word of God?

# CHAPTER 10

## *Are You Part of God's Plan?*

It is always easy to blame God for what is happening in this life without addressing the cause. Men in general always have the tendency to blame someone when things go wrong. But if we were to sit down and ask ourselves a few questions whenever something happens, we would not blame others. What I would like to emphasise today is that no matter who you are, male or female, brown, yellow, black, or white, free or slave, educated or uneducated, dependent or independent, fat or slim, rich or poor, you are unique. You are the only one of your kind. If you were to die today, the world would not find your replacement. No one can accomplish the plan and purpose of God for your life. You are created for a purpose and therefore need to come to that place where you ask God about your part in this world

Jeremiah 29:11-12 put it plainly: *'For I know the plans I have for you, "declares the Lord,plans to prosper you and not to harm you, plans to give you hope and a future". Then you will call upon me and come and pray to me, and I will listen to you.(NIV)* Man for generations has taken for granted God's agenda and replaced it with his own. We need to come back to our maker and ask him where he wants us to be. We have tried to go our own ways and have forsaken what the Lord has set for us. Let's stick to God's plan and we will have the future of God.

Many Christians today are still wondering whether they have been called. If you don't know where you are going, any road will lead there. It is time to find your destination and the direction will come. God has a plan for your life. Let him do the directing. Your ways will lead to death, but God's way will lead to life. He is that God who will lead us to our destination. He doesn't just start or lead us halfway into the journey, but to our destination. Remember that not only are we led to our destination, but in leading he also provides. Let's for a moment consider the plan of God for the prophet Jeremiah.

## THE CALL OF JEREMIAH

Jeremiah 1:4-10 says,

> *Then the word of the Lord came unto me, before I formed thee in the belly I knew thee, and before thou comes forth out of the womb I sanctified thee, and I ordained thee a prophet unto the nations. But the Lord said unto me, say not I am a child, for thou shalt go to all that I shall send thee, and whatsoever I command thee thou shall speak. Be not afraid of their faces: for I am with thee to deliver thee, says the Lord. Then the Lord put forth his hand, and touched my mouth. And the Lord said unto me, Behold, I have put my words in thy mouth. See I have this day set thee over the nations and over the kingdoms, to root out, and pull down, and to destroy, and to throw down, to build, and to plant. (KJV)*

The prophet Jeremiah was a young man when God called him. It is good to bear the yoke at your youth. When God touched the mouth of Jeremiah, who was yet a youth, nothing was said of the purging of his iniquity; because of his tender years he had not so much sin to answer for. No wonder the preacher said in Ecclesiastics 12:1, *'Remember now thy creator in the days of thy youth, while the evil days come not, nor the years draw nigh, when thou shall say; I have no pleasure in them.'* It is always better to seek the Lord early. He needs to instruct you in the things you should do. Don't wait until evil days, when everything surrounding you becomes like a shadow. Seek him when it is day and the light is not grown dim. Seek him before the pitcher is broken at the well. We turn to respond to the call of God only when it suits us and we have nothing else to do; no wonder we do not see the glory of God in our life. We also try to find excuses why we cannot respond to the call. Remember, he is your maker and he knows what is good for his people.

Jeremiah was called when things went well under that good king Josiah, but he continued through all the wicked reigns that followed. In our calling, not only do we need to think that the wind will be fair and favourable, but we also need to know how soon it can turn tempestuous.

Remember, in both situations God has a purpose for you. Jeremiah was called to the house of Jacob to tell them their sins and to warn them of the judgement of God that were coming upon them. Those who adhere to warning and repent receive the mercy of God, but those who do not heed will be destroyed beyond mercy. The very God who ordained and commissioned Jeremiah is the same God who knew him when he was still forming in the belly and was brought forth out of the womb. God is the rightful owner and can therefore employ us into his service as he pleases. Not only was Jeremiah known, but he has also been sanctified and set apart as a prophet unto the nations.

Fear is one of the enemies to God's call. Often we expect thing to go smoothly when we are called. Bread and butter, milk and honey, on the table at all times. We always expect a smooth ride. Have we forgotten that in life there are ups and downs, hills and valleys? The Psalmist put it very plain: 'Many are the afflictions of the righteous, but the Lord delivers him out of them all.' God telling Jeremiah not to be afraid of their faces indicates he would be frightened along the way, but God was with him to deliver him. Not only was he called but he was also told what to say. He that is sent is also instructed and empowered. For without authority to go, how do we do it?

If you are a believer then I would like you to know that not only have you been called by God, but also you have been given authority—a delegated authority. God has power in himself and in turn has delegated this authority to us to go in his name. Jeremiah was set over the nations and over the kingdoms to root out and to pull down. He was sent not as a King to rule but as a prophet who has God's word. He who has the word of God has more power and authority than that of a king, over his kingdom. Men are to be ruled by the word of God, not by the whips of a dictator who desire they please him. Jeremiah was to root out all the evil of the Jewish nation, destroy idolatry and other wickedness and those vicious habits and customs that had long ago taken root. He was to throw down the kingdom of sin.

Jeremiah was to plant the fear of God in their heart and minds. Not only was he to rain down doom on nations, and God would ratify and fulfil it according to his word, but he was also to assure those who repented of their sin that God is faithful enough to forgive them and to cleanse them of all unrighteousness. Jeremiah was to set before them life and death, but he encouraged them to chose life. He was truly given the power to bind and to lose. You are no different! If God was able to do much with Jeremiah, he can do the same with you. Jeremiah had a part to play in the life of his people, and so have you. God is waiting for you to respond. You have to make the most of it.

# ABRAHAM'S CALL

Genesis 12:1-3 states, *'Now the Lord had said unto Abram, Get thee out of thy country and from thy kindred, and from they father's house, unto a land that I will show thee; and I will make of thee a great nation, and I will bless thee, and make thy name great; and thou shalt be a blessing; And I will bless thee, and curse him that curses thee and in thee shall all the families of the earth be blessed.'(KJV)*

The promise of God to Abraham was not only for him and his seed but was also intended ultimately to bring redemption to all mankind. Because of the importance of his promise to God's people, it was repeated three more times to Abraham.

Many would say it was easy for Abraham to respond to the call of God in his life, but I would like you to know that it wasn't easy. This was a man who had lived in his father's house, with his kindred and in his own country all his life. A sudden move was not something he had ever dreamt of.

His father had enough for his family and enough to spare. He had no need to travel, no, not from his kindred, his tribal friends with whom he had grown. Neither did he need to leave his beloved country, Ur, for the unknown. Not only was he instructed to go to the land that he didn't know, but he also had to leave his friends behind.

What surprises did this new land have in store for him? What garnet had he to hook his hope and aspirations on? How could he be so certain that the land would yield the necessary food to support him and his family if he moved? With so many unanswered questions, the verse four of the same chapter says, *'So Abraham departed as the Lord had spoken.'* Abraham did not reason with himself whether he should go, but the scripture says that he departed just as the Lord had spoken.

Romans 4:20-24 (KJV) helps us understand Abraham's actions. It says, *'He staggered not at the promise of God through unbelief, but was strong in faith, giving glory to God; and being fully persuaded, that what he had promised, he was able also to perform.'*

The greatest enemy in the believer's life is unbelief. How many of us are able to run with the call of God in our life without hesitating, giving room to the devil to operate. We doubt the power that is in the word of God, which comes to us. Where is our confidence and our trust in our maker? Abraham's actions speak volumes. He took the promise just as it came to him. He realised the call and was convinced that it took precedence in his life over all other concerns. It was a high calling; the business of the Kingdom needed to be done.

How do you respond to the calling of God for your life? It is time to look out and respond to the call, no matter how big or small it might seem at the beginning. Your response is vital and cannot be taken for granted. Your family, your community, your nation, and maybe the world as a whole may depend on it. It is your calling, not mine. I also have my calling, and I must respond to it. You may not be able to do mine, and I may not be able to do yours. Until each and every one of us accomplishes his or her part, the full blessing that God intended may not be revealed.

Let's take a look at 1 Corinthians 3:6-8. Paul said, *'I have planted, Apollo's watered; but God gave the increase, so then neither he that planted any thing, neither he that waters; but God that gave the increase. Now he that planted and he that waters are one, and every man shall receive his own reward according to his own labour.'* Until you plant and the other waters, the desired increase may not happen. When you and I play our part in the plan of God, the desired increase will surely come. Our failure will hinder us and cause a shortfall in the great reward God has purposed for each and every one of us.

# MOSES' CALLING

Exodus 3:1-9:

> *Now Moses kept the flock of Jethro his father-in-law, the priest of Midian; and he led the flock to the back side of the desert, and came to the mountain of God, even to Horeb. And the angle of the Lord appeared unto him in a flame of fire out of the midst of a bush, and he looked, and beholds, the bush burned with fire, and the bush was not consumed. And Moses said I would now turn aside, to see, God called unto him out of the midst of the bush, and said, Moses, Moses. And he said here am I and he said draws not nigh hither, put off thy shoes from off thy feet; for the place whereon thou stand is holy ground. Moreover he said, I am the God of thy father, the God of Abraham, the God of Isaac, and the God of Jacob. And Moses hid his face, for he was afraid to look upon God.*
>
> *And the Lord said, I have surely seen the affliction of my people which are in Egypt, and have heard their cry by reason of their taskmasters; for I know their sorrows; And I am come down to deliver them out of the hands of the Egyptians, and to bring them up out of that land unto the place of the Canaanites, and the Hittites, and the Amorites, and the Perizzites, and Hivites, and the Jebusites. (KJV)*

During this time in history Moses was minding his own business and not expecting any interference. Surprisingly, this was also the time appointed for God's plan and purpose to be accomplished in his life. The heavenly calling demands attention, irrespective of what we are doing at the moment.

God's call takes precedence. We need to be at the right place at the right time. Until you are called, get your hands on something and pray for the right moment of God to come. The only business worth doing is the Father's, the maker of the heavens and the earth. God saw the affliction of his covenant people, the Israelites, who were in Egypt and therefore need a channel through which he could bring deliverance to them.

You may sometimes wonder why God needs a human channel through which to operate whenever he is about to do something on earth. There is a simple answer to this: God does not want to override our will. When he created the heavens and the earth, he included our input in the things that should happen here. We also need to remember that God is a spirit, and for him to operate in our natural world, he needs a body through which he can operate. One may ask, 'what about the natural phenomena that happened in the bible days, such as flood and pestilence?' If we check the scriptures we will get to realised that before all these phenomena happens God always warn the people or the nation involved. God did not take them for granted. He released the earth lease to man and made man the god of this world. He therefore consulted man before He does anything. He does not over ride men will. This is why Satan became the god of this world when man sin by obeying the serpent in the garden. Man handed his God given authority to Satan in obeying him. Man had God given authority over the earth, this enabled us to rule the earth. Why then do we hesitate when we are called? Why do we disobey when we are instructed? The good of the land comes to those who are willing and obedient. When God saw Israel's sorrows, he needed a vessel through which his children could experience the joy he had in store for them. God saw their sorrows, heard their cries, and witnessed their oppression when the Egyptians oppressed them; the only thing needed was a vessel to send to Pharaoh.

At the time of Israel it was Moses, but today it might be you. It is sometimes easy to single yourself out and blame others. What I would like to call your attention to is that God has seen the suffering, the hunger, the deaths of innocent children, the floods, the fires, the earthquakes, the wars and the rumours of war, but what is left is the vessel, through which he can effect his redemptive plans. If we make ourselves available, he will use us.

We have seen and heard many sorrows and cries; so also has God. Just as he said to Moses, 'Come now therefore, and I will send you unto Pharaoh that thou may bring my people the children of Israel out of Egypt', and he obeyed, so is he calling out to you. When Moses obeyed, many things were accomplished in the lives of Israel. Since God shows no partiality, what he did in the lives of Israel he is capable enough of doing today through your life.

## DANIEL'S CALLING

You may say, 'But I am neither Abraham nor Moses', but you can be Daniel. The part Daniel played in Israel's history is unique. Daniel 9:1-3 says, *'In the first year of Darius the son of Ahasuerus, of the seed of the Medes, which was made king over the realm of the Chaldeans; in the first year of his reign. I Daniel understood by the books the number of the years, whereof the world of the Lord came to Jeremiah the prophet, that he would accomplish seventy years in the desolation's of Jerusalem. And I set my face unto the Lord God, to seek by prayer and supplications, with fasting, and sackcloth, and ashes . . .'(KJV)*

During this time Israel was in captivity, Daniel included. They had become slaves in a strange land. As it was the normal routine of his life to spend time before God in prayer and in reading his word, he was prompted on one occasion, on the word of God, which came to Jeremiah. Our daily walk with the Lord also determines how willing and ready we are to take on the mantel to do the great things of God, for our life, our nation, and the world as a whole. When Daniel spent time meditating on the word of God, from the book of Jeremiah, he understood that God was to accomplish seventy years of desolation in Jerusalem. Having this knowledge, Daniel set himself to seeking the Lord in fasting and in prayer. He come to realise what God could do in the things, that He has promise, and what part he had to play in God's plan. Not only did Daniel pray about the promise of God, but he also requested God not to remember his sins and the sins of his people Israel. Even if you don't feel the calling of God in your life, you surely know you have been called to pray.

Daniel's prayer life resulted in many revelations from God, most of which have been revealed and others yet to be revealed.

# Joshua's Calling

Joshua 1:1-8(KJV)

> *Now after the death of Moses the servant of the Lord, It came to pass, that the Lord spoke unto Joshua the son of Num, Moses minister saying, Moses my servant is dead, now therefore arise, go over this Jordan, thou, and all this people, unto the land which I do give to them, even to the children of Israel.*

> *Every place that the sole of your foot shall tread upon, that I have given unto you, as I said to Moses. From the wilderness and this Lebanon even unto the great river, the river Euphrates, all sun, shall be your coast. There shall not any man be able to stand before thee all the days of thy life: as I was with Moses, so I will be with thee; I will not fail thee, nor forsake thee. Be strong and of a good courage: for unto this people shalt thou divide for an inheritance the land, which I swear unto their fathers to give them. Only be thou strong and very courageous, that thou mayest observe to do according to all the law, which Moses my servant commanded thee; turn not from it to the right hand or to the left, that thou mayest prosper whatsoever thou goes. This book of the law shall not depart out of thy mouth; but thou shall meditate therein day and night, that thou shall make thy way prosperous and then thou shalt have good success.(KJV)*

Every single individual wants to be prosperous and successful, but do we have what it takes? If you are that individual who is so busy, going to and from without spending time in the word of God, it is time you stop, look, and listen. Your success is not in your own hands; it depends on the word of God in you.

The word of God in you can make the difference between life and death, poverty and prosperity, light and darkness. Perhaps due to the death of a relative, husband or wife, mother or father, friend or child, you have given up on life. You may be thinking it's all over, I am done, I am finished. Just for a moment, stop, look, and listen. It is not over yet, neither are you done or finished. Don't count yourself out. Your time will come, and that time is now, but only if you will allow God into the situation. He is willing if you are willing. Weeping and mourning will not bring answers, but your willingness to take God at his word and challenge him will. One word from the Lord is enough to bring you to your inheritance.

Joshua and the whole of Israel were mourning after the death of Moses, the servant of the Lord. They were full of bitterness and anxiety because of his death. Who is going to lead them to the land that the Lord had promised them? It was Moses who had the promise of God and spoke face to face with God, but now he was dead. The man with the mantle, the word, the laws, and the precepts of God was no more. The very man who opened the Red Sea and blocked the Egyptian way with fire, Moses, the man who provided for them both bread when they were hungry and water from the rocks when they became thirsty—who was could bring them to the promised land apart from Moses? This is why God has to emphasised to Israel about his promise to them even though they seem to have lost sight of God's promise to them. God has to reassure them that he was with them, in every place that they would go. God gave Joshua to Israel as a successor to Moses to lead his people to the promised land. Joshua was given the same promise and protection as Moses. Joshua was not going to fail or forsake his people, just Moses would not. The only thing left for Joshua to do was to be strong and courageous. Joshua was not to allow the scriptures to depart from his mouth. This would come about by meditating on the word of God day and night, turning neither left or right.

If we look around us today we see so many men and women who are discouraged due to the inevitable distractions of life. With some, all hope is gone. Remember, you can make the difference. Avail yourself and God will use you for his own glory. They need to get to their destination, and you, like Joshua, need to lead them. When we look at the life of Joshua, we realise that he did not fail, just as God promised him.

## THE FISHERMEN'S CALLING

Matthew 4:18-22: *'And Jesus, walking by the sea of Galilee, saw two brethren, Simon called Peter, and Andrew his brother, casting a net into the sea: for they were fishermen. And he said unto them, follow me and I will make you fishers of men. And they straightaway left their nets and followed him.'* How many of us are able to respond to the call of God, which comes to us? How many times do we close our eyes and ears when we are called? And how many times do we sit idle, waiting for something to happen? The calling of God comes to those who are already involved and have their hands full. Prove to God that you can make it. Peter and Andrew's experience was as fishermen, but the Lord was able to use them for his purpose. No matter who you are, the Lord can use you.

# Paul's Calling

Acts 26:12-18:

*Where upon as I went to Damascus with authority and commission from the chief priest, At midday, O king, I saw in the way a light from heaven, above the brightness of the sun, shining round about me and them which journeyed with me. And when we were all fallen to the earth, I heard a voice speaking unto me, and saying in the Hebrew tongue, Saul, Saul, why persecutes thou me? It is hard for thee to kick against the pricks. And I said, who art thou, Lord? And he said I am Jesus whom thou persecute. But rise, and stand upon thy feet; for I have appeared unto thee for this purpose to make thee a minister and a witness both of these things in the which thou hast seen, and of those things in the which I will appear unto thee; Delivering thee from the people, and from the Gentiles, unto whom now I send thee, To open their eyes, and to turn them from darkness to light, and from the power of Satan unto God, that they may receive forgiveness of sins and inheritance among them which are sanctified by faith that in me. (KJV)*

Paul, as we know, was going about minding his own business. With authority and commission from the priest, he went about persecuting the Church with the view of doing God a service. With the zeal and enthusiasm for the so-called God service, on his way to Damascus he was stricken by the Lord with blindness. As believers, we need to know whose service we are in. We need to check our calling to see if it is of God or of men. If we are not careful, we may be drowned with the principles of this life, thinking it is God.

God's calling always comes with a purpose. When God calls, he instructs, empowers, leads, provides, and accomplishes his purposes in our life. Firstly, the things he wants you to do will be spelled out. God never leaves his children in the dark. He always makes the vision clear to us. Secondly, he makes sure we never fall short of his power, as long as we continue in the things that he has instructed us. Remember, his word alone is even power. It doesn't come out the void of power, but it always accomplishes the purpose for which he sends it. The authority to go on the instructed vision is always given. Thirdly, he leads us, directing us everywhere possible to bring to pass the desired results. Fourthly, he provides everything that is necessary with regard to the vision. God's vision never falls short of his provision. Lastly, he accomplishes his purpose in our lives. Even though the vision may sometime delay it will surly come to pass, so wait for it. At the appointed time, it will happen, if we don't give up. God's vision is destined to come to pass. He who has promised is faithful enough to bring it to pass.

Paul's calling never lacked the provision of God. God equipped him, empowered him, led him, provided for him, and accomplished his purposes in him. With his second letter to Timothy, Paul said, 'I have fought a good fight, I have finished my course, I have kept the faith'. Paul remained focussed and won the race that was set before him. Can we do the same? When he was called, he was not disobedient to the heavenly vision. How often do we try to do our own thing or mingle the things of this world with the heavenly vision. This is what renders the power of God none effective? Paul had to forgo his vision, which was contrary to God's vision. Neither did he confer with any man. Paul's letter to the Galatians reveals more about his success.

Galatians 1:15-16: *'But when it pleased God, who separated me from my mother's womb, and called me by his grace, To reveal his son in me, that I might preach him among the heathen; immediately I conferred not with flesh and blood.'(KJV)*

Let's for a moment consider how Paul saw his calling. (a) Paul saw that no matter how sinful he was, the Lord still loved him.

81

His murders and threats were not taken into consideration. Paul realised that he had been set apart for God's vision, even before he was born. (b) He saw that he had been called by grace and not by any work of righteousness. There was nothing therefore he could take credit for. (c) He realised the purpose of God for his life and how much he desired to reveal himself to him. He saw that this revelation had come about so as to enable him to preach him among the Gentiles. (d) When he realised the importance of the calling, Paul did not confer with flesh and blood.

Believers need to know where we stand in relation to the calling of God in our life. There is so much to be done. The challenge had been thrown to us all. How do you respond? Are you one of those who turns a blind eye? Remember, there are things to be done; there are visions to be accomplished. Just as Paul, Jeremiah and others were known before they were born to accomplish God's purposes—are you so known? Remember, God is no respecter of persons, neither does he show any partiality.

Believers are called for great and mighty things, and not just churchgoers and pew warmers. We are called not only to the light of the Lord but also to be the light of the world. In people's darkness we need to shine. In their hopeless situation we need to have hope. We have to make known to the world the love of God for all mankind. We need to preach the good news to the entire world, and as we go, signs shall follow those that believe. Remember, until we go, signs and wonders will not follow. Seek your part in the Kingdom's business and the world be liberated.

# CHAPTER 11

## *God Given Access to Himself*

I was brought up by a father who lived with a second wife in another town whilst my mother and her children lived in another town. Only occasionally did I see or visit my father. He was somebody who, to my knowledge of him, didn't say much, but always meant what he said. The only time I had the chance to talk to him was when we were travelling from one town to another. I stood a better chance of getting more communication from him if I was alone with him. That was the only time I had most of his attention. At other times all the children would be around, and every one of us would be trying to have the best chance to communicate or ask questions. It was very precious time for me, having the opportunity to speak to my dad.

I grew up not knowing much about my dad, and therefore I ended up having many unanswered questions. Life, therefore, held many uncertainties for me as I grew up. I therefore needed to come to that place where I realised the importance of communication in a relationship. Where there is love and intimacy, there will always be proper communication in the relationship.

Our relationship with God should always have that proper communication needed to keep the fire alive in our life. Prayer is that fire that keeps our relationship with God alive with all power. A prayer-less Christian will always be powerless in his or her relationship with God. Your relationship with God determines your dependency. Your dependency is also determined by your prayer life. The Church has a wonderful Father who would neither leave us nor forsake us.

In Jeremiah 33:3, he says, *'Call unto me, and I will answer thee, and show thee great and mighty things, which thou know not.'* Oh! What an open door to the Father of glory, with whom there is no limitation. There is no time limit or busy schedules with God. At anytime and everywhere and for whatever purpose, he will answer and show us great and mighty things we know not. Not only do we get the things we pray for, but things are revealed to us. He is not like that earthly dad who responds when he feels like. With God, all his promises are always *yes,* but we are the ones to say Amen to the glory of God. There is no limit to what God can do when we pray.

## HEZEKIAH'S PRAYER

2 Kings 20:1-6 says,

*In those days was Hezekiah sick unto death. And the prophet Isaiah the son of Amos came to him, and said unto him 'Thus says the Lord, Set your house in order; for thou shall die, and not live. Then he turned his face to the wall, and prayed unto the Lord, saying, I beseech thee, O Lord, remember now how I have walked before thee in truth and with a perfect heart, and have done that which is good in thy sight. And Hezekiah wept sore. And it came to pass, afore Isaiah was gone out into the middle court, that the word of the Lord came to him, saying, Turn again, and tell Hezekiah the captain of my people, thus says the lord, the God of David thy father, I have heard thy prayer, I have seen thy tears: behold, I will heal thee: on the third day thou shall go up unto the house of the Lord. And I will add unto thy day's fifteen years; and I will deliver thee and this city out of the hand of the king of Assyria; and I will defend this city for mine own sake, and for my servant David's sake. (KJV)*

Hezekiah could not be intimidated by his sickness or the message that came to him from the prophet Isaiah. The only focus was on God, his maker. Having realised who God was and what he is capable of when his children call upon him, the only option left for him was to turn to his maker, with whom he has a closer relationship, to present his case. When he prayed, the situation was turned round. We need to realise that Hezekiah did not complain or go about telling people about his conditions to men or women, as we sometimes do when we have problems. He remembered that God is the one who has the whole world in his hands and can turn situation around. Men and women can fail and discourage you and even talk you down, but God will not when you turn to him in prayer.

Hezekiah began to reason with God through prayer. He called to mind his covenant and his walk with God, both in truth and with perfect heart. He also called to mind the good he had done in the sight of God.

This is one of the old Testament stories in which God changes his mind, taking more lenient course of action in response to man's plea. The secret was Hezekiah's prayer. Our prayers bring God to the scene to intervene in the things that man, by himself, cannot control. Your prayer can make the difference. Christians should not only believe but also act on what we believe.

We not only have our faith in Christ, but our life is also in him. As the root is in the soil, the branch in the vine, the fish in the sea and the oceans, the bird in the air, so the life of the spirit-filled believer in Christ Jesus our Lord. We know that Hezekiah was the captain of God's people, with whom he was in covenant. Not only did God answer the prayers of Hezekiah, but he also remembered the covenant. It is a mutual obligation, a solemn oath between God and his chosen people, where there is both blessing and curses with blood as a seal and a guarantee. God never breaks his covenant promises to his people; neither does he forget his people when they call to him.

In Jeremiah 33:3 God spoke through the prophet Jeremiah, *'Call upon me, and I will answer thee, and show thee great and mighty things, which thou knows not.'* Yes, he is our maker. He formed and established us, and above all he covenanted with us so as to receive unto ourselves his blessings and his glory.

Our prayers remind we can rely upon his promises. In our prayers we remind God of our absolute dependency on him. In prayers we say to him that we, by ourselves, cannot make it. It is in prayers that we call God to intervene on our behalf for the things that we are naturally unable to change.

It is in prayer that we agree with Paul's writing that in him we live, we move, and we have our being. We try to make it by our self, but we fail miserably and fall flat on our faces.

## David's Prayer

There is no greater challenge to us than that of David. The man the scriptures says specifically that, he was the man of God's own heart. His life says it all. Does this mean that David was someone special? Why was he successful above all his contemporaries? Even when it came to choosing a king, he was the unlikely choice. Samuel might have well been looking for someone tall and handsome, but he was chosen and prepared by God to be a leader of his people.

Was David successful due to his leadership? The answer is obviously no, because not all leaders are successful. David's prayer life makes the difference. So also is your prayer life for your success or your failure. David is a man who, when he fought Goliath and won the victory, did not attribute it to his own abilities but to the power of God, with whom he was in covenant. When David behaved himself wisely in all his ways, the Lord was with him.

1 Chronicles 14:8-11a says, '*And when the philistines heard that David was anointed king over all Israel, all the Philistines went up to seek David. And David heard of it, and went out against them. And the Philistines came and spread themselves in the valley of Rephaim. And David inquired of God. Saying, shall I go up against the Philistines? And will thou deliver them into mine hand? And the Lord said unto him go up; for I will deliver them into thine hand. So they came up to Baal-perazim; and David smote them there.*'(KJV)

David here did not turn to live in the past, knowing perfectly well the history of his victory over the Philistines even before he became a king over Israel. He did not just jump on them when they came against him. It is so easy to rely on our past glory and achievement and turn our back to the Lord, but not so with David. The scriptures say he did inquire of the Lord whether or not to go up against the Philistines.

He also inquired if they were going to be delivered into his hands. He did remember who his source was. Victory comes neither by might nor by power but his spirit. How often we as men turn to depend on our own might and power and later realise our mistakes after falling flat on our face.

The same story continues from verse 12-17:

> *And when they had left their gods there, David gave commandment, and they were burned with fire. And the Philistines yet again spread themselves*

*abroad in the valley. Therefore David inquired again of God; and God said unto him, goes not up after them; turn away from them, and come upon them over against the mulberry trees. And it shall be when thou shall hear a sound of going in the top of the mulberry trees, that then thou shall go out to battle: for God is gone forth before thee to smite the host of the Philistine. David therefore did as God commanded him: and they smote the host of the Philistines from Gibeon even to Gazer.*

This passage helps us to understand how much of God's directions we do need in our lives. Not only did David seek God, but he was also ready to obey the command that God gave him. It is one thing to pray, but it is another to wait on God to carry on the command that is given. Victory comes to those who will seek the will of God always and will be able to obey fully the instructions they are given.

It was made clear to the prophet Isaiah that if we are willing and obedient we will eat the good of the land. David smote the Philistines, from Gibeon to Gazer due to his willingness, his obedience and his, dependency on God. The good of the land comes to those who are willing and obedient to God's word.

How much of God do you seek in your daily life? What percentage of your affairs with men and women, with your family and community, with your nation and other nations, do you present to God in prayer daily? I strongly believe that God will not do something until someone prays. Your prayer will make the difference in the society in which we live. It took prayer for the hostages that were held in Afghanistan to be released. In the things we allow God to lead, he will always provide.

# Jabez's Prayer

1 Chronicles 4:9-10 (KJV) says, *'And Jabez was more honourable than his brethren; and his mother called his name Jabez, saying, because I bear him with sorrow. And Jabez called on the God of Israel, saying. Oh that thou would bless me indeed, and enlarge my coast, and that your hand might be with me, and that thou would keep me from evil, that it may not grieve me! And God granted him that which he requested.'*

Jabez prayed one of the most important prayers of the Bible. Being born in sorrow due to some difficulties his mother went through, Jabez did not allow that to intimidate him. He went on his knees to seek the God, with whom his people Israel were in covenant, to change the situation round. There are four important requests Jabez made from God in his prayers. The first was that the Lord would bless him. Blessing is something that we as believers need to seek of the Lord. We are not told why Jabez was more honourable than his brethren were; could it be because the scribes dwelt at Jabez that he was more learned and pious. I do personally believe that it was due to his inclination to devotion, which made him truly honourable, and by prayer he obtained those blessings from God that added much to his honour.

The way to be truly great and truly good in all areas of your life is to put aside much time for prayer. Jabez was so keen for God to bless him knowing perfectly well that his blessing would come from the Lord and not from men. Many people find it very difficult to ask God to bless them. We know perfectly well that he that is redeemed of the Lord is blessed. Yes, we are blessed, but we need to apply this blessing to our lives. When we breathe in air, we need to open our nose or mouth to allow it into our lungs to work in our system. When we close our mouth and our nose, the air will not be able to flow for the purpose it is required. What am I saying? We need to ask God if we want to be blessed. He does not override our will. Just as we go to the shop to buy what we want, so also do we need to ask for the thing we need for this life. Jabez asked for blessings and he was truly blessed.

Secondly, he prayed that the Lord would enlarge his territory. The Lord said to both Moses and Joshua, every place that the soles of your feet tread upon that land have I given to you. So also did God give to Abraham his territory to operate in the blessing that God has bestowed upon him. It is God on whom our expansion depends. Are you that individual looking for expansion in business, in your Church, and in your life? Then ask God like Jabez did to enlarge your territory in all these areas and that good God will bless and enlarge you.

Thirdly, he prayed that the hand of the Lord would be with him. Our promise is that the Lord will not leave us nor forsake us, but how often do we turn to come out of the umbrella of God's protection because of our sins? The Psalmist says, 'he that dwells in the shelter of the most high will rest in the shadow of the Almighty.'

Jabez' prayers indicate his desire for God's constant protection upon his life. It was like David, saying, 'The Lord is my shepherd. I shall not want.' His dependency is of God. His security is of God. Jabez prayed that he couldn't do it by himself, but with the Lord's intervention. Remember, what you receive will depend on how much you depend on your God.

Lastly, he prayed that he would keep him from harm so that he would be free from pain. The promise to the Church from the head, in Isaiah 54:17, is that *'no weapon forged against you will prevail, and you will refute every tongue that accuses you'*. It is a promise for God's heritage, but we need to live under that promise, appropriating it into our system. It is one thing knowing the promise, but it is another applying it to our lives. In Hebrews

11:6, the scripture says, *'And without faith it is impossible to please God, because anyone who comes to him must believe that he exists and that he rewards those who earnestly seek him.'* Jabez prayed that he might not depart from the faith.

It is lack of faith that keeps us out of God's protection. If his faith remains intact, he will be kept from harm which brings pains. Like sickness and many other pains that believers suffer, it is from the devil. If you live outside sin you live outside pain. Sin opens the door to the devil. Close the door and the devil has no way in. Let us keep our focus on what James wrote in chapter four, verse seven: *'Submit yourselves, then, to God. Resist the devil, and he would flee from you. (NIV)'*

Jabez prayed for God to help him keep his part of the bargain, and he would be free from pain.

## JESUS TEACHES ON PRAYER

Our life of prayer is very important in Christendom. Prayer will always keep us focussed. We cannot make it without it. Mark 9:14-29 says,

*"When they came to the other disciples; they saw a large crowd around them and the teachers of the law arguing with them. As soon as all the people saw Jesus, they were overwhelmed with wonder and run to greet him." What are you arguing with them about? "He asked. A man in the crowd answered, "Teacher, I brought you my son, who is possessed by a spirit that has robbed him of his speech. Whenever it seizes him, it throws him to the ground. He foams at the mouth, gnashes his teeth and become rigid. I asked your disciples to drive out the spirit, but they could not." "O unbelieving generation", Jesus replied, how long shall I stay with you? How long shall I put up with you? Bring the boy to me." So they brought him. When the spirit saw*

*Jesus, it immediately threw the boy into convulsion. He fell to the ground and rolled around, foaming at the mouth. Jesus asked the boy's father, "How long has he been like this?" "From childhood," he answered." It has often thrown him into fire or water to kill him." But if you can do anything, take pity on us and help us" "if you can?" Said Jesus, "Everything is possible for him who believes." Immediately the boy's father exclaimed," I do believe; help me overcome my unbelief." When Jesus saw that a crowd was running to the scene, he rebuked the evil spirit. You deaf and mute spirit" he said "I command you, come out of him and never enter him again." The spirit shrieked, convulsed him violently and came out. The boy looked so much like corpse that many said; "He's dead," But Jesus took him by the hand lifted him to his feet, and he stood up. After Jesus had gone indoors, his disciples asked him privately, why couldn't we drive it out? He replied, "This kind can come out only by prayer". (NIV)*

Most often when we read this passage of the Bible we tend to think how weak and powerless the disciples were. In the same way, we sometimes get discouraged when we don't get results in some areas of our lives.

Here Jesus reveals why we do not receive when they pray. When we pray the right way we would receive answers. We need to have a desire, pray, believe and we would receive. Our prayers release the power of God on our behalf to bring to pass the desired purposes. The world expects much from us. How are we going to give what we don't have? We can give to the world what it is lacking in this life only through prayers. Prayer opens the door for God to work in our situation. With prayers, we can change the world.

## DANIEL'S PRAYER

One of the men of God who prayed for things to happen was Daniel. He was a man who prayed no matter the circumstances.

He prayed even if it killed him. When Nebuchadnezzar besieged Judah, he took young men in whom there was no blemish, good looking, gifted in wisdom, possessing knowledge and quick to understand back to his kingdom. He made them to serve in his palace. They were to be taught the language and literature of the Chaldeans. It was with this group of people of which Daniel and his companions were part. Daniel and his friends did not forget their God. They separated themselves from the delicacies of the king choices of food and drink which was offered to their gods. When they kept themselves pure and holy to their God, the scripture says, God gave them knowledge and skill in all literature and wisdom, and to Daniel understanding in all vision and dreams.

Daniel's prayer life brought deliverance from the king's firm decision of destruction, not only for himself and his friends but also for the astrologers, the magicians, the wise men, and the soothsayers at Nebuchadnezzar's palace and kingdom as a whole. Daniel 2:17-19 (KJV) says, *'Then Daniel went to his house, and made the decision known to Hananiah, Mishael, and Azariah, his companies, that they might seek mercies from the God of heaven concerning this secret, so that Daniel and his companions might not perish with the rest of the wise men of Babylon. Then the secret was revealed to Daniel in a night vision. So Daniel blessed the God of heaven.'*

This is one of the secrets of getting results from prayer of faith. Daniel and his companions were not intimidated by what was going on around them in Babylon. They knew who they believed and therefore were not going to allow fear to determine their circumstances. There was a decree of death awaiting all the wise men of Babylon, including them. Daniel knew the importance of prayer, so he called his friends together to pray to the God of heaven. When they sought the mercies of God concerning the secret, it was revealed to them. Not only did they receive revelation concerning the secret, but things that would come to pass during the end time were also made known to them. When we made God our prayer partner, he made known to us the hidden thing that was not known. He fulfilled his word, which he spoke to the prophet Jeremiah, that we should call unto him and he would answer us and show us great and mighty things that we did not know. This is exactly what happened in the life of Daniel and his friend.

We would be living in the dark if we were to stop praying. They that make God their friend in prayer receive revelation as their reward. We come to know the will of God in our prayer. The world in which we live in today needs light, but the only way this revelation can come to light is through your prayer and mine. Nebuchadnezzar came to know God as the God of gods, the Lord of kings, and a revealer of secrets. Through our prayer, the Lord will bring salvation to the world, and kings will also come to the knowledge of God.

Not only in the reign of Nebuchadnezzar of Babylon when Daniel held public office did he realise the importance of prayer, but also in the reign of Darius of Mede. When Darius began his reign he set one hundred and twenty satraps over the whole kingdom. He also set three governors over the satraps, and Daniel was one of them. With an excellent spirit, Daniel distinguished himself above the governors and the satraps. He was faithful both to God and to men, with no error found in him. Out of envy, the governors, the administrators, the satraps, the councillors, and the advisers compelled the governor to make a decree by which they might trap Daniel, humiliate him, and finally kill him. What I personally want you to realise here is that, as a believer, your faith is always under attack. The only thing the devil is after from a believer is your faith. We please God with our faith and we fight the enemy with our faith. Without our faith, we have a problem. The leaders tried to attack Daniel's faith, but he stood on the word of God, which brought him victory. He relied on the word of God and exercised his faith through prayer. As usual, Daniel realising the plans of the enemy, opened his window—as always facing Jerusalem, the city of his God—and prayed. Here he was found and brought before the king.

Daniel 6:16 (NKJV) says, *'So the king gave command, and they brought Daniel and cast him into the den of the lions. But the king spoke, saying to Daniel "Your God, whom you serve continually, he will deliver you."* Our faith will be tried always, but how many of us can pass the test? This passage tells us how Daniel was able to pass the test, living us with one of the greatest testimonies of the Bible. In the den the hungry lions could not lay any mark on Daniel, so as to eat him up. When we spend time in prayer knowing whom we have believed, we will see the glory of God.

Daniel 9:2-4 (NIV) says, *'In the first year of his reign, I Daniel understood from the scriptures, according to the word of the Lord given to Jeremiah the prophet, that the desolation of Jerusalem would last seventy years. So I turned to the lord God and pleaded with him in prayer and petition, in fasting, and in sackcloth and ashes prayed to the Lord my God and confessed.'*

Having come to know the plan of God for his people from his word, he prayed and reminded God of his promise. It should not surprise us, that we still need to ask God for the things that He has promised. God does not override our will. Even though he has promised, we are the ones to say Amen to the glory of God. Our appreciation of what he has provided takes place through prayer of thanksgiving.

When we remember who we are in relationship with God, then we will know how to pray correctly. Daniel did call to mind the awesomeness of God and his covenant of love with his people—how he brought his people from the land Egypt with a mighty hand and they sinned against him. How many of us are able to count the blessings of the living God when we receive them in our lives?

Daniel 9:20-23:

> *While I was speaking and praying, confessing my sin and the sin of my people Israel and making my request to the Lord my God for his holy hill, while I was still in prayer, Gabriel, the man I had seen in the earlier vision, came to me in swift flight about the time of the evening sacrifice. He instructed me and said to me. Daniel I have now come to give you insight and understanding. As soon as you began to pray, an answer was given, which I have come to tell you, for you are highly esteemed. Therefore consider the message and understand the vision. (NIV)*

Through his prayer, the angel was assigned to deliver swiftly to Daniel the plan and purpose of God for Israel and the world as a whole. He received the massage of the lord and a vision was given to him. This vision was relevant not only to Israel but to the world as a whole. The revelation of the Lord comes to those who spend time in the word and in prayer. Prayer opens our hearts and minds to the things of God, which in the natural would be impossible to apprehend. Daniel was very highly esteemed. Prayer is the element of life that brings us to the place where we can see the perfect will of God. In Daniel's prayer the end-time prophecies were given and explained.

My dad could not give me all the answers that I needed, but the Holy Spirit power in prayer can. Prayer can turn most of our situations around. We should also remember that problems will come, persecutions will arise, we will sometimes suffer lack, troubles and hardship may also come, but with prayer, victory will be received. Where we allow God to lead, he will surely guide.

# CHAPTER 12

## *God Brings Us to Our Provision*

Often we find it difficult to understand why we suffer lack. We always expect things to be available wherever and whenever we want. Not only do we want our needs to be met, but also we always desire to have more and for life to be exceedingly abundant. The natural man is full of greed, which is idolatry. We desire to have more than we have not because it is insufficient but because others have more.

Some kill to acquire more, some rob others, some steal to increase their portion, some lie to get more—no matter what it takes the covetous man or woman will devise a way to get more.

Proverbs 14:12 says, *'There is a way, which seems right to a man but its end is the way of death.'*

Men over the years have tried to do things by their own power and failed miserably. Man's way leads to death, but God's way leads to life and peace through Christ, who quickens us. It sometimes looks as though the men of the world are winning, but thank God those who seek God diligently in every area of their life will reign in this life. We acquire wealth and we think it is by our own power. Yet Deuteronomy 8:18 declares, *'But thou shall remember the Lord your God, for it is he who gives you power to get wealth, that he may establish his covenant which he swore to your fathers, as it is this day.'(KJV)*

Believers should come to that place where they know that they by themselves cannot make it, no matter how much they try. If we leave out God, we fall flat on our faces.

Ecclesiastics 9:11 says, *'I returned and saw under the sun that the race is not to the swift, nor the battle to the strong, nor bread to the wise, nor riches to men of understanding, nor favour to men of skill, but time and chance happen to them all.'* All our works are in the hands of God. The world event will always contradict the prospect we have of them when we operate outside the will of God. All praises should go back to God when we receive the things we ask for. We will only be what God say we are.

## ISRAEL IN THE WILDERNESS

God did not take Israel to the land of promise by the direct route. God not only wanted them to see his mighty work, but he wanted them to depend on him for their sustenance. Not only were they supposed to go to the land of Canaan, but God also wanted to get Egypt out of them. They needed to understand that God alone was their provider and that nothing could be accomplished by their own strength and power. They needed to depend on God throughout their journey with God, both in the wilderness and in the promised land. History declares that the Lord was with them in all areas of their life. In chapter 16 of the book of Exodus we see how Israel needed to call on God for their sustenance. It says in verse 2,

> *Then the whole congregation of the children of Israel complained against Moses and Aaron in the wilderness, And the children of Israel said to them, Oh, that we had died by the hand of the Lord in the land of Egypt, when we sat by the pots of meat and when we eat bread to the full! For you have brought us into the wilderness to kill this whole assembly with hunger. Then the Lord said to Moses, behold, I will rain bread from*

*heaven for you. And the people shall go out and gather a certain quota every day, that I may test them, whether they will walk in my law or not. (NKJV)*

God needed to prove to Israel that he was capable of providing them with food and drink, just as he was able to deliver them from the hands of Pharaoh and from the land of Egypt.

Verses 16-18 say, *'This is the things which the Lord has commanded, let every man gather it according to each one's need, one omer for each person, according to the number of persons, let every man take for those who are in his tent. And the children of Israel did so and gathered some more and some less. So when they measured it by omers, he who gathered much had nothing over, and he who gathered little had no lack. Every man had gathered according to each one's need.'*

I would like everyone who is reading this book to realise the awesomeness of the God we serve. He is the one who provides our needs according to his riches in glory by Christ Jesus. It is our needs that he supplies, not our greediness. Those men of Israel who tried to have more than others ended up having the same amount as others;, a single omer apiece. No one had more than what had been assigned. How many times do we try to be first and end up being last? It is what God gives us which is a blessing, not what we acquire by our own power. The arm of the flesh shall fail us.

Verses 19 and 20 say, *'And Moses said, let no one leave any of it till morning, Not withstanding they did not heed Moses. But some of them left part of it until morning and it bred worms and stank. And Moses was angry with them.'*

Believers are sometimes like Israel in our everyday dealings with God. We lay up treasures for the worms. Our churches may be in need of finances to reach the unsaved, the poor, and the destitute.

But all the spare money would be sitting in the bank, where only the very few would benefit from it. Our pastors would be doing secular jobs to earn a living, but the so-called believer would not be paying their tithes to keep food in the storehouse of God. Where is our obedience to the word of God? Malachi says we rob God of both tithes and offerings. Let what is provided for us today always be sufficient for today. Tomorrow will provide for itself. We turn to focus on the things of the flesh so much that we forget to live by faith. Anything that is done outside faith is sin. Our faith in God brings us to our inheritance. Israel needed to have faith in the God who was their deliverer—for the water they had to drink, the food they had to eat, and every basic necessity. God had to prove to them that if he was able to bring them out of the land of Egypt, and that he was equally capable of providing for their needs.

Christians need to consider their position in Christ. Not only are we saved, but we are also blessed. Salvation comes with a package, and the moment we enter into that covenant relationship with God that package is handed to us. Some of the goodies we receive in the package of salvation include healing, prosperity, redemption, propitiation, righteousness, and many more. Our true union with Christ will bring all these advantages to pass. When Christ was admonishing his disciples, he asked them to seek the Kingdom of God and its righteousness first and all others would be added. Israel had to learn that the God who defeated the Egyptian army and brought them safely out of slavery would provide the necessary water for life by the same power, for he changes not. Time and time again, God had to take Israel through faith-building excises. One step at a time he helps us to grow in faith.

The way their needs were provided was so unique. The manna, which was the bread from heaven, came six days a week and was absent on the seventh day, which constituted the day of rest, or the Sabbath. Whatever was left each day was destroyed by worms after the morning gathering. But on the sixth day Israel was able to gather a double portion. They baked or boil what they would eat for the day, and they laid up the rest until morning for Sabbath day, and it did not stink; neither were there any worms in it. Where God leads there is always provision and protection. Israel came to understand that they needed to depend on God every day of their lives. Verse 35 says, *'And the children of Israel did eat manna forty years, until they came to a land inhabited:they did eat manna, until they came unto the borders of the land of Canaan.'* For forty years they depended on God. Our everyday life should be dependent on God. We need nothing more and nothing less. We will surely make it to our destination if our faith is rooted and grounded in the word of God.

## ABRAHAM, THE MAN FROM UR OF THE CHALDEES

In order for us to come to the provision of God, we need to know how to respond to his call, his love, and his grace. Our dreams and visions will not happen overnight. The vision is for an appointed time, but it will surely come to pass if we faint not. Our faith is the vehicle that transports us to the destination of our vision.

Hebrews 11:8(NKJV) reads, *'By faith Abraham obeyed when he was called to go out to the place which he would afterward receive as an inheritance. And he went out, not knowing where he was going. By faith he sojourned in the land of promise as in a foreign country dwelling in tents with Isaac and Jacob, the heirs with him of the same promise, for he waited for the city which has foundations, whose builder and maker is God.'*

Abraham moved in obedience when the calling of God came to him. He was not reluctant to the divine call of God as some of us do. He obeyed and moved from Ur of the Chaldees in

Mesopotamia to the city of Haran north of Palestine. Even though Haran was not the intended city of God, he made a move all the same, until such time that the word of God came back to him. Not only did Abraham have faith, but it was a growing one. Our faith needs to grow to take on board all that the Father has in store for us. Instead of leaving home alone to the promised land, the scriptures say he left with his father, Terah, his wife, Sarai, and his nephew, Lot. When the word of God came back to him, his imperfect faith became growing faith, since he responded again to the divine call. He was commanded to leave all and go out into the unknown, where he would be sustained only by the promise of God. The scriptures declare that he left not knowing where he was going. He waited for the city, whose builder and maker was God. He desired a city which had a strong foundation. When he finally made it to Canaan, Abraham couldn't stay because of famine that came on the land. His imperfect faith moved him to the land of Egypt, but he couldn't shake off the promise of God in his life. Like Abraham, many of us are quickly shaken by the circumstances of this life, and we deviate from the vision of God for our life. Not only did Abraham need to go back to Canaan, but he also need a separate himself from his family, since until now Lot was still in his company. He was afraid not only of lack but also of loneliness.

Genesis 13:14 (KJV) says, *'And the Lord said to Abram after that Lot was separated from him, Lift up now thin eyes, and look from the place where thou art northward, and southward, and eastward, and westward; for all the Land which thou sees, to thee will I give it and to thy seed for every.'*

His growing faith allowed him to see himself as the man set apart for God. God's promise was given not only to Abraham but to his seed also. Not only was he promised a land but also a nation. This happened because Abraham began to grow in faith. We will clearly see the directions to the vision of God when we continue to walk in faith. Verses 21 and 22 of chapter 14 of the book of Genesis also help us to see Abraham's dependency on God. He opposed the king of Sodom's demand and the wealth of the world, knowing clearly that his protection and his provision came from God. Giving tithes of all to Melchizedek, the king of Salem, after his victory over the kings, indicated his acknowledgement of God as his strength and protector. What belongs to God should be given to him with no strings attached, and in return he will repay us as promised.

Chapter 15:1-6 (KJV) of Genesis indicates where our growing faith can lead us. It says,

> *After these things the word of the Lord came unto Abram in a vision, saying Fear not, Abram, I am thy shield, and thy exceeding great reward. And Abram said, Lord God, what wilt thou give me seeing I go childless and the steward of my house is this Eliezer of Damascus? And Abraham said, Behold to me thou hast given no seed; and, lo one born in my house is mine heir. And behold, the word of the Lord came unto him, saying, this shall not be thine heir; but he that shall come forth out of thin own bowels shall be thin heir. And he brought him forth abroad and said, look now toward heaven and tell the stars, if thou be able to number them; and he said unto him, so shall thy seed be. And he believed in the Lord, and he counted it to him for righteousness.*

When Abraham walked in faith he was declared righteous. He was not sure to have the nation since he had no rightful heir., but hearing the word of God caused his faith to rise and increase in his life. Paul, writing to the Romans, said faith comes by hearing, and hearing comes by the word of God. Sometimes looking at our circumstances causes fear to arise and intimidate us, but if we look to the word of God then faith will arise. God is our shield and our reward. We should note that Abraham's righteousness was accounted to him before he was personally circumcised as a sign of his covenant with God, and even before the law was given four hundred years later. Circumcision and the law have nothing to do with our righteousness. God continues to seek those who will trust, obey, and have confidence in him through complete obedience to his son, Jesus Christ. It is that kind of faith that God accepts as a substitute of perfect righteousness. It was through Abraham's growing faith that God began to give a preview of the events yet to come.

Verses 13-21 explain how God cut a covenant with Abraham and also how his descendents would be strangers in a foreign land for four hundred years. They were not only going to be strangers, but they were going to serve and be afflicted all those years. God also promises to judge the nation and deliver them after four hundred years in captivity. He promise to bring them to their own land. God spell out the dimensions of the land he was going to give Abraham and his descendants. Today when believers go through trials and difficulties for a short time they turn to give up thinking the Lord has forsaken them. Abraham and his descendant have to wait for four hundred years for the promise to come to pass. Abraham knew the end from the beginning and was not discouraged but counted him faithful that has promised. Their bondage in Egypt was part of God's plan. Your future is also in the plans of God.

Jeremiah 29:11(KJV) says, *'For I know the thoughts that I think toward you, says the Lord, thoughts of peace, and not of evil, to give you an expected end.'*

Our destiny is in his hands, if we submit to his sovereign love. We should remember that there is no testimony without tests or trials. At the end of the tunnel there shall be light, just as there was in Abraham's covenant with God.

Verse 17 says, *'And it came to pass, that, when the sun went down, and it was dark, behold a smoking furnace, and a burning lamp that passed between those pieces.'*

In whatever darkness we find ourselves in, as believers we need to remember that God is capable of bringing to pass the desired light.

Genesis 17:1:5 *says,*

> *And when Abraham was ninety years old and nine, the Lord appeared to Abram, and said unto him, I am the Almighty God, walk before me, and be thou perfect. And I will make my covenant between thee and me and will multiply thee exceedingly. And Abram fell on his face; and God talked with him saying. As for me, my covenant is with thee, and thou shall be a father of many nations. Neither shall thy name any more be called Abram, but thy name shall be Abraham; for a father of many nations have I made thee. (KJV)*

Believers like Abraham try to help God bring his promises to pass. But who are we to help God? His wife Sarah is past the years of child bearing. He himself is growing older each day, and he is already ninety-nine years old. Abraham and his wife were tired of waiting for the promise of God to be fulfilled, so they went to Hagar the Egyptian handmaid. The proceeds for their lack of faith was Ishmael, the son of the bondwoman. Our faith should rest in the promise of God and not in our own power. Abraham and his wife's sin and discouragement made God reaffirm his covenant promises to them. God affirmed his promise to Abraham that he should continue to walk before him and he would be perfect. God is our perfecta. For God to bring Abraham to that level of mature faith, he had to change Abraham's name from exalted father to father of a multitude, stirring in them new capacities with their new names. The Lord also reaffirmed his covenant promises to prove to them the seriousness of his calling and his provision in their life. He also gave them the covenant of circumcision so that in looking in their body they could therefore say, yes, our covenant God is able to bring to pass his promises. The seal of his covenant with God was therefore the circumcision of his flesh. Believers today are called to circumcise our hearts, in other words, to cut off our fleshly nature, which draws us back into the world. After the new name, the circumcision, and the reaffirmation of the promise of God to Abraham and his wife, the scriptures indicate the growth and maturity in the faith of Abraham.

Romans 4:17-21 says,

*(As it is written, I have made thee a father of many nations,) before him, whom he believes, even God, who quickeneth the death, and calleth those things, which be not as though they were. Who against hope believe in hope, that he might become the father of many nations, according to that which was spoken, so shall thy seed be. And being not weak in faith, he considered not his own body now dead, when he was about a hundred years old, neither yet the deadness of Sara's womb. He staggered not at the promise of God through unbelief, but was strong in faith, giving glory to God. And being fully persuaded, that what he had promised, he was able also to perform. (KJV)*

The passage here helps us to understand the extend of Abraham's faith. This happened when Abraham's faith had matured, not allowing unbelief to set in. He did not look at his circumstances, nor at his wife Sarah's old age, but at God, who had promised. Abraham believed even though there was no tangible reason to do so. He did not allow the things that he saw, heard, and sense intimidate him from becoming the father of many nations.

God's promise of perfection comes to those who mature in faith. This can happen only when we lay aside every weight and sin, which so easily besets us and entangles us, and focus on Jesus. Abraham learned his lessons in a very hard way. It is not easy to give up your own son, but Abraham had to do it for the promises of God to come to pass. It should be God's way, not men's, his plans and not our plans, his future and not our future. It is God's will and not our will.

Through faith and patience, God's promise came to pass. Genesis 21:1-2 says, *'And the Lord visited Sarah as he had said, and the Lord did unto Sarah as he had spoken For Sarah conceived and bore Abraham a son in his old age, at the set time of which God had spoken to him.'* We always need to know that what God has promised will come to pass, for he is faithful.

Abraham's promises did not come to pass overnight; there was a period of waiting. We inherit the promise with faith and patience. After the promise there were still more tests to go through. For his faith to be perfected he needed to pass these tests. A gift had been given. The expected promise had been fulfilled. Was Abraham going to nurse the gift and forget about the giver and the provider, just as we sometimes do in our Christian race? Some come expecting, but as soon as they receive, they then disappear from the Church and sometime give up their Christianity.

Some also give up when the provision is delayed in coming, causing them to go out and seek alternatives. It is only those who hang in there that receive the promise.

Genesis 22:1-2: *'Now it came to pass after these things that God tested Abraham, and said to him, Abraham! And he said, here I am. And he said, Take now your son, your only son Isaac, whom you love, and go to the land of Moriah, and offer him there as a burnt offering on one of the mountain of which I shall tell you.' (NKJV)*

Abraham was asked to offer his son Isaac as a sign that he still had faith in the God who provided him with Isaac. With two other servants and Isaac, Abraham headed to the mountain of God. Verses 4-7 of the same chapter say,

> *Then on the third day, Abraham lifted his eyes and saw the place afar off. And Abraham said to his young men stay here with the donkey, the lad and I will go yonder and worship, and we would come back to you. So Abraham took the wood of the burnt offering and laid it on Isaac his son. Then he took the fire in his hand and the two of them went together. But Isaac spoke to Abraham his father and said, my father, and he said, here I am, my son, and he said look, the fire and the wood, but where is the lamb for the burnt offering. And Abraham said, my son, God will provide for himself the lamb for a burnt offering.*

This brings us to the mature side of Abraham that God is seeking from all believers, not only Abraham. Abraham had so many cattle and herds out of which he could have selected to sacrifice to the Lord. We even read from the passage that he had servants from whom one could be taken in place of his son. Even though servants could apply to the position of prime minister, none could take the place of a son. Abraham had not only Eliezer but also other slaves. Should I behave like the nations from which I have been drawn from? Who offer his sons as sacrifice to his gods? What is special about Isaac? I was all right without Isaac, because I had my Ishmael. Why give him and then request him of my hand? This and many more questions I believe went through the mind of Abraham. With all this confrontation, Abraham's faith was still in God, who called him to a land first, to a nation second, and to many nations third. Is God still your focus after the thing you have been through? He still had faith in God that even if he offered his son God would be capable of resurrecting him. Abraham statement to the servants, that, 'he and the lad would go and worship and come back' indicate his faith in the God who has instructed him. His statement of faith also says it all. My son, God will provide himself a lamb for the burnt offering. He departed as God has commanded him, not wavering, knowing that with God all things are possible, and that where he leads he always make a way and provides.

Abraham came to know that the Lord is the Jehovah (*jirah*), but he learnt it in a very hard way. He learnt that God when a need arises God was able to provide. It is only those who are mature in faith who see the glory of the Lord. It is only by faith and through faith that we receive the provisions of God.

## ISAAC'S BLESSINGS AT GERAR

Genesis 26:1-6

> *There was famine in the land, beside the first famine that was in the days of Abraham. And Isaac went to Abimelech king of the Philistines, in Gerar. Then the Lord appeared to him and said, do not go down to Egypt, dwell in the land of which I shall tell you. Sojourn in this land, and I will be with you and bless you, for to you and your descendants I give all these lands, and I will perform the oath, which I swore to Abraham your father. And I will make your descendants multiply as the stars of heaven, I will give to your descendants all these lands, and in your seed all the nations of the earth shall be blessed, because Abraham obeyed my voice and kept my charge, my commandment, my statutes, and my laws. So Isaac dwelt in Gerar. (NKJV)*

This was a time of need for Isaac, who needed to feed not only himself but also his flock and his servants. With no food around to sustain him, his only bet was to move to Egypt, just as his father did when famine broke out in the same land. But God told to him not to go to Egypt but to stay in Gerar, where he would be blessed. What a test of faith! How many of us would be able to stand this test and pass? We who are in covenant with God need to understand our covenant partner. For he is able to make a way where there is no way. It is not what our fathers did that is important, nor what our friends are doing, nor our selfish motives, but rather what the Lord is saying to you. Isaac had to stay not only because it was the Promised Land but also because the Lord reaffirmed his covenant blessing to him. The word of God is full of covenant promises and blessings for the believer. When Isaac was admonished not to move to Egypt, he obeyed. It is the provider whom we need to seek, not the provisions.

Verses 12-16 of the same chapter continues, *'Then Isaac sowed in that land, and reaped in the same year a hundredfold, and the Lord blessed him.'*

Isaac, in obedience, began to prosper and continued prospering until he became very prosperous. Isaac had possessions of flocks and herds and a great number of servants. So the Philistines envied him. Now the Philistines had stopped up all the wells, which his father's servants had dug, and they filled them with earth. And Abimelech said to Isaac, 'Go away from us, for you are much mightier than we.'

Who said God can't change your situation around? If we are obedient to his word we will always eat the good of the land. Isaac did not sit back and become sluggards but began to do something to bring to pass God's blessing in his life.

Against all odds Isaac sowed, not considering the hardness of the soil or its bareness. He looked unto God who has promised him. By himself Isaac was not able to change the situation that was confronting him, but by looking unto God, there was hope. He therefore trusted God knowing that he was able to deliver what he has promised. The land, which had failed everyone and brought much hardship to the people of Gerar, became a land of blessing to the man of God. God was his promise and provider. In Isaac's obedience, the scriptures declare that not only did he prosper and continue prospering, but he became very prosperous, so much so that the Philistines began to envy him. Remember, God is able to bring you to the same level of prosperity if you are obedient to his word.

Abimelech and his people couldn't stand Isaac and his riches, because he became mightier than all, and he even compelled him to leave in the interest of peace. We need to remember that it will not be everyone who would be happy when you get a blessing from God. But we shouldn't be intimidated by that, for it is God who bless and when he bless no one can curse. No one can touch God's anointed. Your own friends will sometimes desert you. Don't be discouraged because of that, for the Lord himself is your friend and will give you friends who will come to know his power.

## WATER FOR THE HOST OF ISRAEL AND JUDAH

This was the time the king of Israel, the king of Judah, and the king of Edom came against the king of Moab, as a result of the king of Moab's rebellion against the king of Israel. To them Moab was a common enemy. Before they saw the faces of their enemies they were all in danger of perishing for want of water. They marched through the wilderness, the very place where their fathers had much food to eat and water to drink. The very common commodity had reduced the army of these three kings to nothing.

The scriptures indicate that they fetched a compass for a seven-day journey, and there was no water for the host and the cattle that followed them. This situation actually humbled these three kings and brought them to a place in search of God. They remembered what their fathers told them concerning the land on which they were in need of water, how the Lord opened the rocks and gave them water to drink. This may have triggered their desire to seek the God of their fathers. They consulted God through Elisha the prophet. Just like these three kings, we only call on God when we try and fail instead of seeking his face in our daily endeavours. He is our God and maker, and there is nothing hidden from his sight. When Elisha was consulted, the hand of the Lord came upon him, and he instructed these three kings.

2 Kings 3:16-20 says,

> *And he said, thus says the Lord, Make this valley full of ditches. For thus says the Lord, you shall not see wind, nor shall you see rain; yet that valley shall be filled with water, so that you, your cattle, and your animals may drink. And this is but a trivial thing in the sight of the Lord. He will deliver the Moabites into your hand. Also you shall attack every fortified city and every choice city, and shall cut down every good tree, and stop up every spring of water, and ruin every good piece of the land with stones. Now it happened in the morning, when the grain offering was offered, that suddenly water came by the way of Edom, and the land was filled with water.( NKJV)*

These three kings' faith was tried to establish if they truly sought the Lord.

They were made to make ditches to receive the water. If we seek the blessings of God we need to make room for them. Not only did the Lord promise to fill the ditches with water, but there would be enough for all and their cattle. He said to them there shall be neither wind nor rain, but they shall have water. I want you to remember that he is the same God whom we serve today. God always seeks our obedience. He has not changed since the days of our fathers, and neither shall he today. To the kings' amazement the valley where they made their trenches was filled with water, but there was neither wind nor rain. Those who sincerely seek the dew of God's word will always have their desires met. Not only were they saved from perishing for lack of water but they were also assured of victory over their enemy.

## Elijah the Desert Dweller

1 Kings 17:1-6 says,

> *And Elijah the Tishbite, of the inhabitants of Gilead, said to Ahab, as the Lord God of Israel lives, before whom I stand, there shall not be dew nor rain these years except at my word. Then the word of the Lord came to him saying, 'Get away from here and turn eastward, and hide by the Brook Cherith, which flows into the Jordan. And it will be that you shall drink from the brook, and I have commanded the ravens to feed you there! So he went and did according to the word of the Lord, for he went and stayed by the brook Cherith, which flows into the Jordan. The ravens brought him bread and meat in the morning, and bread and meat in the evening, and he drank from the brook. (NKJV)*

This is one of the most fascinating pieces of history in the scriptures. We read it, and we begin to wonder how he did it. Where does Elijah come from? Who were his mother and father? He seems to drop in out of nowhere.

The Jews might fancy him to be an angel from heaven, like Melchizedek, with no beginning and no end. The disciple James described him as a man like any one of us. The record we have here indicates he was a Tishbite, which means a desert dweller. If his lifestyle had been like that of John the Baptist, Elijah might have been feeding on locusts and wild honey. He dropped in at the time when Israel had turned its back on the Lord. He was the God who had been their provider and giver, just as he had for their fathers. Ahab the king had turned the heart of men and women of Israel to the worship of Baal, the pagan god. A nation is under the wrath of God when it sins, and Israel was no different.

Elijah prophesied that there would be no rain for three and half years. We may ask why a word form a man out of nowhere should carry such weight. Remember, the scripture declares that a fervent prayer of righteous man avails much. God shows no partially, and neither is he a respecter of persons. Elijah was no different from any of us.

Our faith in God is what makes the difference. After his prayer, the Bible says God spoke to him and directed him. He was instructed to go to the Brook Cherith, where ravens would feed him and he would drink from the brook. If it was you and I it might have been a very difficult move. It might have been impossible. We may have questioned why ravens, since they are birds of prey. Yet Elijah did not think that the food they brought would be unclean, but he received it and gave thanks to the Lord. Ravens are birds that naturally do not feed their young, yet when the Lord pleases he makes them feed his prophets.

Ravens bring little and broken meat at a time, but when it comes to his prophets he is able to make them bring wholesome meals. They who wait on the Lord shall have their strength renewed and be satisfied when the needs arise. Our God will always provide when we let him lead. Even when the brook dried up, God kept providing for his prophet. God's miracles come to those who prepare for them. When the heavens fail the earth also fails. The heavens fail those who come out of the umbrella of God's provision. It is he who dwells in the secret place of the most high who would abide in the shadow of the Almighty. Depend on God and he will be your source.

*1 Kings 17:8-9 says, 'And the word of the Lord came unto him saying, arise, get to Zarephath, which belong to Zidon, and dwell there, behold, I have commanded a widow woman there to sustain thee.'( NKJV)*

Surely it takes faith to walk with God. His ways are not our ways, and neither is his thought our thought. Paul says God has chosen the foolish things of this world to confound the wise. First ravens, then a widow to sustain Elijah. In our obedience, not only do we receive the blessing of God but also those who will come with us. Inasmuch as God provides for Elijah, the widow also flourishes with God's blessing. The widow had more for herself and also for her two sons—not only for a day but until rain came down for the ground to yield its fullness. A widow at the time Elijah needed to be fed by the family or the community if the family cannot fulfil that responsibility. To no one was the Prophet Elijah sent to than a widow to sustain him. God is able to turn our lack into abundance and our weakness into strength. He is able to turn our situation around.

Matthew 14:13-20 says,

> *When Jesus heard it, he departed from there by boat to a deserted place by himself. But when the multitudes heard it, they followed Him on foot from the cities. And when Jesus went out he saw a great multitude, and he was moved with compassion for them, and healed their sick. When it was evening, His disciples came to him, saying, this is a deserted place, and the hour is already late. Send the multitude away, that they may go into the village and buy themselves food. But Jesus said to them, they do not need to go away. You give them something to eat. And they said to Him we have here only five loaves and two fish. He said bring them here to me. Then he commanded the multitudes to sit down on the grass. And he took the five loaves and two fish, and looking up to heaven, he blessed and broke and gives the loaves to the disciples, and the disciples gave to the multitudes. So they all ate and were filled, and they took up twelve baskets full of the fragments that remained. Now those who had eaten were about five thousand men besides women and children.(NKJV)*

This was the time Jesus and the disciples set themselves apart to a deserted place to rest after grieving for John the Baptist. They set themselves apart to rest, but the people travelled on foot to find the site even before Jesus landed. These were people who were desperate for the spiritual things of God. They that reach out for the things of the spirit will also be given the things of the flesh. The Lord, seeing the multitude, realised that they were like sheep without a shepherd, and he was moved with compassion for them. No matter how much we are deserted, the spirit of the Lord is able to draw us to himself, where his provision will abound more and more. The disciples, realising the need of the people, requested the Lord Jesus to send them away to go and fend for themselves.

Man in his effort to help others would ask that they work a little harder or try a little more. But with the heart of compassion the Lord said to them, 'You give them to eat.' It was the disciples who were to provide for the people. Where we see need we must provide. We have the God-given power to provide for the needy. If we have power over evil spirits then we need to know that we also have authority over famine and destitution. We also have power over those who turn people into slaves, and also power that make laws that bring economic hardship to the lives of many millions of people whom God have created in his own image and after his likeness. Authority is given to the believer to bring to earth the God given blessings. We don't need to look at our lack but at he that is able to increase and multiply the little that we have.

The Lord took the only five loaves and two fishes that they had an blessed them. Miraculously the disciples were able to feed the five thousand men besides the women and children. We need to realise that if we keep what we have to ourselves there shall be no increase, but if we entrust it into the hands of the Lord we will see the increase. A closed hand cannot be filled, but when we open our hands to the needy, the Lord will cause our increase to come. It will not be limited, but press down, shaking together and running over. When you give, it will open the door to the supernatural manifestation of God for your life.

A story in the book of second book of Kings indicates how a widow with two sons came to Elisha to help her from the creditors who had come to take her sons away to be his slaves. The widow had nothing except a jar of oil. The man of God asked her to go and borrow from his neighbours' empty vessels, lock herself at home, and begin to pour it into the vessel. The vessels were supernaturally filled as she became obedient to the word of the man of God.

How much do you have? It doesn't matter how big or small, the Lord is able to bring the increase. The widow of the sons of the prophets in the days of the prophet Elisha received the increase of her oil as she became obedient. She had enough to sell to pay her debts and enough to feed herself and her two sons. A jar of oil increased to pay all her debts and provided enough to depend on for many days until the rains returned. Just as the five loaves and two fishes increased to feed five thousand men, so also did the oil increase in the Shunammite widow's life. We need to seek the provider and not the provision. The increase is of the Lord and not man, or we ourselves.

# CHAPTER 13

## *God-Given Authority*

Man was created in the image and likeness of God and given power over everything that God created. When creation was completed by God the responsibility of keeping and tending the garden and all the creative things were lift in the hands of Adam the man of God. As long as man reasons with God, he will be able to fulfil his God-given responsibility.

Matthew 18:18 puts it very simply: *'Assuredly, I say to you whatever you bind on earth will be bound in heaven, and whatever you loose on earth will be loosed in heaven.'*

A believer's authority does not depend on who we are but to whom we belong. Our God-given authority is within reach. What we bind on earth we bind in heaven. The angels of God are always on assignment to carry our instructions through. The only way to implement our God-given authority is to speak it. If we speak it, it will surely come to pass. When a seed is grown it germinates and bears fruits. It can be neither good nor bad. What is sown is what we reap. A good seed will produce good fruit and a bad seed will produce bad fruit. By their fruit we shall know them. I do find it difficult to hear people saying, 'It doesn't work for me.' The problem here is that many people are not sowing but do expect to reap. Many are sowing the wrong seed but do expect to reap the right fruits.

Many believers, instead of praying for God's intervention in their situation, only sit down and say, 'God will do it' or 'God knows my situation.' It is true that God can do it, and it is equally right that he knows the problems, but until we entrust it into his hands God will do nothing about it. We all know that when a seed is sown it germinates and bear fruits, but if the seed is not sown, would it bear fruits? The answer is obviously that it cannot. The field or the ground needs to be prepared, and then the seed sown for the right results can be achieved. Keep your seed or eat your seed and there will be no increase.

Many believers today are living on yesterday's confession. Their life today was their past declaration. What we sow today will be our harvest tomorrow. What many people don't seem to understand is why certain things happens in their life. But there are answers to every question that life throw at us. Every seed sown would always produce the fruit that is required. Believers therefore need to watch what they are saying, since it will produce the required fruits.

Jesus himself explained the principle of sowing and reaping.

Mark 4:26-28: *'And he said, so is the kingdom of God, as if a man should cast seed into the ground; and should sleep, and rise night and day, and the seed should spring and grow up, he knoweth not how. For the earth bringeth forth fruit of herself; first the blade, then the ear, after that the full corn in the ear.' (KJV)*

The principle behind the seed bringing forth in its season has already been put in place within God's own natural law. Just as men cast seed on the ground and know not how it comes up, so also is the Kingdom's principles. The word of our mouth works with the same principle that Jesus indicated in the verse 14 of the same chapter of the book of Mark. *The sower sows the word.*

The word that comes out of our lips is seed. And any seed sown will germinate and also bear fruit. The fruit that it brings forth would be in him. Meaning what we sow we reap, the full corn in the ear, or the full desire. In most cases it is not what we require that comes, but we also need to realised that this was what we sowed. When we sow faith-filled words we will reap the blessings of God. When we sow fear-filled words we will reap things that bring fear and intimidation.

Scriptures make it clear that out of the abundance of the heart the mouth will speak. What is in our heart is the spiritual seed that, when we sow will bring forth its kind. If it is faith it brings forth the spiritual blessings of God. If it is a fear-filled word it will bring fear-filled fruits. This is the more reason why believers need to fill their heart and mind with the word of God for faith to abound, so as to produce faith-filled words whenever we are confronted with situations and trials. If there is no word indwelling, there will be no faith but fear. Many today are saying what the devil is saying instead of what God is saying. When you speak in line with what the devil is saying, you reap what the devil brings, but when you speak what God is saying you reap what God provides. What do you say when you are confronted with a situation? Or what do you say when you don't like what you hear? Do you speak in line with the word of God or with the word of this world? There should be a distinction between a child of God and the man of this world. The man of the world speaks in line with the world, but the child of God speaks in line with what the word of God says. It is what God says that brings the victory that God provides. It is with the mouth that we sow in the Kingdom of God. Sow what you want and it will come to pass.

The Gospel of Luke 1:38 helps us to understand the power of words. It says, *'And Mary said, Behold the handmaid of the lord; be it unto me according to thy word . . .'*

This was the time that the angel of the Lord appeared to Mary with the news that she would conceive in her womb and bring forth a son and call his name Jesus. Looking at her circumstances, that was impossible, since she had known no man. Knowing the power of God in his word, she agreed to the message of the angle that was spoken to her. She trusted that God was able to bring to pass what He has promised. She truly brought forth a child, and his name was Jesus.

In verse 48 of the same chapter she said from henceforth all generations shall call her blessed. And behold and truly all men call her blessed Mary. Not because she is more important than anyone that was living at that time but because she spoke in agreement with the word of God. She regarded him that was going to do those things as mighty, and that he is capable of doing great things. Zechariah on the other hand doubted the word of God that came to him, and as a result of that he became dumb until the promise of God came to pass.

How do you see God and his word? Remember God is watching over his word to perform. It is agreement to the word which brings the desired result nothing more and nothing less. If God is mighty in your life, your marriage, your job, your education, your business he will surely show himself mighty. But if we trust in the things of this world it would surely from this world we will reap. Remember the devil is the God of this world. To speak his language is to remain in his domain.

In Hebrews 4:12 (KJV) it says, *'For the word of God is quick and powerful, and sharper than any two-edged sword, piercing even to the dividing asunder of soul and spirit, and of the joints and marrow, and is a discerner of the thoughts and intents of the heart.'*

It is the word of God that is powerful. The word in believers' mouths is able to do more and exceedingly. As I said, it is only the faith in you that the devil is after. When he touches your faith, then he is able to turn and twist your whole life. Don't give in your faith and the victory would always be yours.

The man who said I can't and the one who said I can are both right. The moment that you say you can't, you shut your brain and stop it from thinking. But the one who says I can allows the brain to work for him to the level where one is able to plan and execute the desired purposes to bring fulfilment.

# CHAPTER 14

## *God-Given Opportunity*

How clearly do we want God to direct and bless us? It is only where he leads that we can hold him responsible when things go wrong or his promises are not kept. God is ready to keep his part of the bargain if we keep our part. Most believers have no clear agenda from which they plan their life. We always expect God to bless us, but as to where, how, and when we ourselves do not know.

One can make a census of a hundred believers with the question, what do you want God to do for you? When do you want him to do it? And how do you want him to do it? I can promise you that only 10 percent of the people can give you clear and concrete answers. The other 90 percent will not be able to tell you, because they don't know what they need from the Lord. This proves that they don't know where they are and even where they are going. Just for a moment, try to answer these question for yourself, and then you will realised that it is not an easy question.

Do you need success? Then plan for success. This question remains unanswered because of our lack of vision and dreams. What is your ultimate goal in life? This will surely determine you success level. Your vision or dream, plus your planning plus your determination and persistency, is what will yield the success that you require.

*First,* let God know what you desire or what your dream is. Remember, dreams are for an appointed time. Lack of clear sense of direction can also cause your success to be impeded.

Habakkuk 2:2-3: *'Write the vision and make it plain on table, that he may run that readth it. For the vision is yet for an appointed time but at the end it shall speak, and not lie. Though it tarry wait for it; because it will surely come, it will not terry.'*

Our dreams need to be written down. This keeps us focussed on working at it each day, in other to bring it to fulfilment. This calls for planning and adjustment where necessary. It is only when we know what we want from the Lord that we know how to pray for and then receive it.

Psalm 37:5: Commit your ways to the Lord and he shall bring it to pass.

*Second*, we need to realise that our *vision also can come to pass with much business, as indicted in the book of Ecclesiastes 5:3.*

You cannot sleep all day and all night and expect to increase overnight. Just ask yourself if there is anything that comes out of nothing. It is what you put in that will grow and increase. What you sow is obviously what you will reap, but with increase, which is God's law of sowing and reaping. If we choose to lazy about then we will truly realise the amount of wrinkles we have on our face. When we arise with God we will surely shine. Christ will arise with us if that is the direction we want to go. When we arise with Christ then all our enemies will scatter.

Proverb 10:4a (KJV): *'He becameth poor that dealeth s with a slack hand.'*

The hand that is not put to good use never experiences the abundance of God. We believers have the God-given ability to succeed and prosper.

Matthew 25:29: '*For unto everyone that have shall be given and he shall have abundance, but from him that have not shall be taken away even that which he has.*'

We need to put our talent to good use and the blessing of God will bring the increase. Either we increase what we have or lose it altogether. You have a dream; therefore, let it come to pass.

*Third*, fear of losing and failure will prevent our vision from coming to pass. We need to allow faith to arise within us to bring to fulfilment of our dreams. If fear arises it sophisticates our faith in our vision. If the vision has been committed into God's hands then surely he is capable of bringing it to pass. A person who fears hinders himself from receiving what God has ordained to be his.

James says God has not given us the spirit of fear but of love and sound mind. With love and sound mind we can approach God and lay hold on the things he has ordained for us. There is none that can stop us. God did not promise us failure but success. He did not promise us that it would be impossible but rather that all things are possible to them that believe. When we come out of fear and allow faith to arise, then we become recipient to the things we demand from God.

When Jericho was strictly shut up because of the fear of the children of Israel, and none went out and none came in, they were taken over by Israel. Fear took away all their resistance, their boldness, and even their strategy. Fear destroys our God-given ability to resist the intruder and also our ability to stand firm and acquire his blessing unto ourselves. Fear destroys our thinking, and without thinking our plans are in jeopardy. Fear brings believers to a place where we accept failure instead of victory, which comes most of the time through persistence.

We have this wonderful promise in the book of Isaiah 41:10 (KJV) *'Fear thou not, for I am with thee; be not dismayed; for I am thy God; I will strengthen thee; yea, I will help thee; yea, I will uphold thee with the right hand of my righteousness.'*

Our strength comes from God and not from men or ourselves. We need to remember that the natural is always aided by the spiritual. Our help is not of men but of God. Men promise and fail, but God is not a man that he should lie. Whatever he has promised he is capable enough to bring to pass. With faith and not fear we receive the things that we desire. Failure cannot cope with persistence.

Isaiah 41 verses 17 and 18 would help us understand this more: *'When the poor and needy seek water and there is none, and their tongue faileth for thirst, I the Lord will hear them, I the God of Israel will not forsake them. I will open rivers in high places and fountains in the midst of the valleys. I will make the wilderness a pool of water, and the dry land spring of water.'*

He is capable of turning our situation around if we keep depending on him. God can bring victory in our failure. The land of En Gedi in Israel today can remind believers today what God can do when our situation becomes unbearable. En Gedi is still a vivid slash of green on the barren coast of the Dead Sea. Here one can swim beneath the waterfall in Nahol David. This is the place where God hid David when he ran away from Saul. It was here that David's God provided for him out of nowhere. Yes, he can surely make a pool of water in our wilderness if we let faith arise in us from his word. He is the one that has redeemed us and called us by name. Wherever we are, God will be with us. The river will not overflow us, and the fire that burns will not consume us; neither can the flame kindle upon us. Jesus promises us that he will be with us even unto the end of the world. The end has not yet come, so let's rest assured that the Lord is with us.

*Fourth*, unchecked bad habits also draw us back. Most Christians turns to procrastinate instead of seizing on the opportunity when it comes. Until we arise and do, nothing will happen. When seed time comes and we decide to wait, all that we will realise next will be harvest time and we will not have sown. The worst thing I hear some people say is that God will do it. But the question is what have you entrusted into his hands to do? Yes, Jesus can do it, but until we show him the vision or our desire, nothing will happen. When God revealed himself to the prophet Jeremiah, God promise that he would hasten his word to perform it. God put his word into the mouth of Jeremiah so He can watch over it to perform when he speaks it. It is the word of God that when spoken in faith which brings result. The word of God given to him took flesh and manifested among men that all might know that he is God. When we speak to the dry bones, God will cause flesh to come and cover them. When we command the four winds of the earth, breath will come upon the flesh and cause them to live.

Hebrews 12:1-2 helps us to understand this more: by saying *'Wherefore seeing we also are compass about with so great a cloud of witness let us lay aside every weight and sin which doth so easily beset us and let us run with patience the race that is set before us. Looking unto Jesus the author and finisher of our faith.'*

Most believers have no time to wait for fruit of their labour. The race set before us requires patience. But how many of us are able to hang in there when things don't go the way we want? Those we see who are successful are the ones who hung in there without giving up when they first failed. Persistency is the weapon that we use to break the backbone of an unbearable situation. With persistency the kings grant to the criminal his wishes.

*Fifth*, arrogance, which is ego and ignorance, destroys one's vision and desire. What one knows will make him successful, but what he doesn't know will destroy him. There is always the need to acquire more knowledge. For lack of it we are destroyed. For Paul to be able to do, there was the need to learn and know. The need for believers to succeed and prosper is now. Where there is the need to study or to take up part-time cause to acquire knowledge, please, let's do it. We are living in a service-oriented society. The services you give bring in the results you expect. Some services require training, but let's do it. We always turn to use the disciples of Jesus as a sort of consolation for not pursuing in education, thinking they were unlearned and ignorant. We need to remember that it was the Jews who saw them to be unlearned and ignorant. So much was done by the disciples, whom the so-called well-educated Jews were not able to apprehend. It is not what we know that matters but what we do in particular with what we know. Start with whatever knowledge you have at your command, and as you go along, acquire better knowledge by sharing what you have. As the disciples walked with the Lord, the knowledge of him increased so much that they were able to prove to the leaders of Jerusalem that they had something extra that the leaders did not have. That something extra is what one requires to make the difference between making it and losing it altogether.

*Sixth*, being humble doesn't necessarily mean we are inferior, but that we are different. Many believers today are sick of inferiority complex, which has reduced them to nothing but dust. They have allowed themselves to be kicked like a football. We all see how Jesus was bold in his dealings with the teachers of the law. He humbled himself unto death, even death on the cross. Humility is not stupidity. It is a level where we commit to the ordnance of God in love and respect for who God is. It is the spirit of boldness that arises within us to claim the things that God has given us. It belongs to us; therefore, let us take hold of it. A negative personality will not induce cooperation. Bad habits like overeating, over drinking, and overindulgence in sex can equally affect all our successes and prosperity, and lack of exercise deprives us of good health.

We have so many issues that are outside our control. The gate to our past is securely shut, with no one to open it for us. Tomorrow is not yet, and therefore we cannot do anything about it. What you and I can influence is *today*. The decision and action we take today will, however, influence our tomorrow and give us a favourable past.

There is a race to be won, with strength at hand, there is a battle to be fought with the victory already given, and there is a blessing to be received, with the way shown. But this and many more will come only to those who are ready to mount on wings like the eagles and run the race set before us and not be weary. We must walk and not faint. For He that is with us, is greater than he that is with them.